Birdsong, Barks, and Banter

Adventures of an Animal Intuitive Reiki Master

and Her Home of Misfit Companions

SHIRL KNOBLOCH

Birdsong, Barks, and Banter: Adventures of an Animal Intuitive Reiki Master and Her Home of Misfit Companions

© Shirley Knobloch, 2012

All rights reserved

IBSN 13: 978-0-9885171-0-3

Special acknowledgement and thanks to my children. To Jennifer, your grammatical skills have been put to good use as my editor. You helped transform my unique style of dangling and dotted thoughts into an acceptable collage of commas, periods, and semi-colons. Thanks, Jen, for understanding a mother's obsessive need to put thoughts into written word and for your constant belief in my ability to do so. To Rebecca, kind friend to feral cats everywhere. No hungry little waif need suffer if he finds a way to your door. And to Stephen, the "Pied Piper" of lost dogs. Strays find you, or you find them, and even in the midst of pouring rain, you will leave your comfort to comfort them.

I am proud that by living amongst a zoo, and in spite of complaints about doing so, my children have formed loving hearts and bonds with all fellow creatures.

Table of Contents

Prologue

Part One: My Journey Begins

The Birds Didn't Answer…Yet	5
You Can't Run Away from Fate	9
Wolf at My Door	11
The Energy that Lingers After Death	21
Do Pets Possess Souls That Live On?	24
Do Dogs See Spirits?	29
Skippy's Story	31
Peter Pan	36
Reiki Finds Me	38
Gretchen	40
The Priceless Look on a Vet's Face	45
Cats Like Reiki—and Birds, Too	47
Dakota	49

Part Two: Embracing "Misfits"

Little Guy	54
Greyfriars Bobby Blue	59
Anthony	62
Angel	65
Apache Tears	67

Casper LambBear Highlander	70
Bram	73
Gingersnap	76
Tad (The Heart Compares)	79
Ozzy (Nine Days of Love)	84
Do Animals Feel Grief?	89
Buddy	92
Smokey	95
Bailey Gargoyle, My Alien Pom	99
Close Encounters of the Fourth Kind (Life with Bailey)	102
Mr. Jingles	105
Val	108
Silver Belle, Buttons, Bunny, and Chip	110
A Christmas Eve Birth	114
Canaries	117
Midnight	120
Friend	122
Chickens Get Rescued, Too	124

Part Three: Spiritual Snippets

Charm	127
Winged Messengers	130

The Oldest Pet Cemetery	133
The Paths of Assisi	136

Part Four: Final Thoughts

Bringing Reiki Home	139
The Value of Reiki	142
Gratitude	147

Epilogue

Everyone has a calling. I know mine is to share my life with the dying. To hold them in my arms, to tell them they are loved, to guide them when the Universe calls them home. I have shared my home with many of them and met many more along my journey as a Reiki Master. I hope my story comforts those who have held loved ones in their arms, as well, before the last time their eyes stared up with love. This book is dedicated to all old dogs over there, gazing at the stars……..

>
> Stare
> Stare
> Stare at the stars and dream, old dog
>
> The glare of the morning sky is harsh
> On those tired, whitened orbs
>
> But the moon is soft
> She welcomes you
>
> Her light beckons
>
> Home
> Infinity of Love
>
> So
>
> Stare
> Stare
> Stare at the Stars
>
> They spread Luna's light beacon
> Lighting the Bridge
> Stare
> Stare
>
> The Stars are the Universe's Diamonds
> Adorning the Hands of Eternity
> Hands that Embrace
> In Love
>
> -- Shirl Knobloch

Prologue

"If I grow fur and pee on the floor...will you love me more?"

Growing up, I always loved the Christmas cartoon *Rudolph*, especially the Island of Misfit Toys. I always wanted to adopt them all—the polka-dotted elephant, the misfit Jack-in-the-Box, all of them. I suppose my dreams came true; I share my home with misfit companions, full of fur balls, feathers, mischief, and mayhem.

This prologue quote pays special homage to the one furless being who shares my home—my husband, Steve. Somehow, he got dragged into this menagerie, living in a zoo of squawks and barks and birdsong.

He once asked, "If I grow fur and pee on the floor, will you love me more?" Funny words, though sad as well, for they voiced a tinge of sorrow I understood and always remembered. He knows he shares my life with many; I come as a package deal, often trailing fur and feathers alongside and on my clothing as I journey amongst the misfits.

My home is a haven for misfits—small, big, young, old, furry, feathered misfits of many varieties and afflictions. All of them vying for a piece of my heart and attention and restricting his access to more of mine.

Most have been old gents in their 70s, 80s, and beyond. Their eyes clouded with cataracts, their muzzles whitened, their fur sparse and balding in some places. To me, they are the most handsome; they reach a place in my heart to which no new puppy can hope to attach, and they Velcro themselves permanently there.

But these old gents need a lot of special care and attention, so I must give thanks for the assistance my furless mate provides. Without his help, I could not set up refuge for a house of misfits. At three or four in the morning, when an old man's bladder has exhausted its limit for the night, it is my husband who gets up and goes downstairs to let him out. When those bladders have night-time accidents, it is he who awakens with chores of pee clean-up duty to help lighten the burden of the remaining day for me.

My husband's brow furrows in bewilderment as I comb through my old man matchmaking sites, a.k.a. rescue pages, looking for new adoptees. When I give donations to others, he asks, "Look around, don't we have our own animal hospice and rescue? Who is donating to us?"

And he is right. It is expensive to care and feed all. Besides being the maintenance man for vomit and accidents of older, ailing dogs, he is the provider who hauls a cartload of special food, treats, and supplements from the pet store home. He is the one who leaves work at night to retreat to a *peaceful* home of barks, mayhem, and mischief.

Without his help, this work would be overwhelming, both physically and financially impossible for me. So, I open this book with the word *Thanks*.

You don't have to grow fur or pee on the floor; I love you already. I know it is difficult to share your home and attention with a menagerie of misfits.

Hopefully, one day, when we have grown older and grey and become misfits ourselves, our children will see that our needs are met with as much care. One thing they need not contend with is all the fur balls. I think we are both safe from growing them, unless I happen to adopt a misfit werewolf. You never know, I have adopted most everything else.

Part One

My Journey Begins

- One -
The Birds Didn't Answer...Yet

My story begins in a small New Jersey suburb. I was a quiet child, the recurring question from all my teachers being, "Why doesn't she smile?" I think I was born old. I believe some of us are old souls incarnate, bringing hidden ancient wisdom and quietness that makes us old when we are young. Newer souls enter this world with a zest and passion for play and mischief; old souls prefer to sit quietly in our rooms and read or draw. In my case, this also included experimentation in the process of telepathy. I discovered my thoughts could be intercepted and transmitted by, and to, others.

I truly feel the most gifted animal communicators are those who have experienced deep hurt and sorrow from childhood, whether they choose to admit it or not. This draws them to the gentle nature and energy of animals where hurt and criticism are not to be encountered or endured. When I had my Reiki practice in New Jersey, I taught workshops in animal communication. I always told my students, quite honestly, that they could expand on their talents, but no one would leave the workshop talking to his/her pets like Dr. Doolittle. Some are born with a genuine gift that just cannot be conjured in workshops or books.

I never told anyone about my telepathic experimentations, probably because I did not know about such energy and occurrences. At least my new body didn't. Somewhere, deep within, my old spirit remembered. Many believe we know our life calling from the time of early childhood. It is those childhood play fantasies—being a heroic fireman or a graceful dancer—that lay quietly inside us, waiting to come to fruition.

I read in *Ripley's Believe It or Not,* one of my favorite books as a child, about a little girl in England who, for a few short years, could step outside and call the wild birds to her shoulder. To me, there was nothing quite as magical on this earth. I remember sticking my head out of my bedroom window, singing and calling to the birds. They didn't come. Eventually, I stopped and let the dream diminish, or so I thought. But inner dreams don't die. Their fires may extinguish and smolder inside if not supplied with passion's fuel, but they remain hidden, asleep, like Sleeping Beauty. They wait, sometimes decades, for that kiss of life; sometimes, sadly, the kiss never comes.

I was the youngest child; many years separated me from my two brothers. When I grew up, pets were not allowed in my home. We had guppies in the living room; my mother would tend to them. I remember, as a youngster, walking into the living room and finding a guppy on the carpet. The force of the filter had ejected her onto the floor. She was pregnant.

My mother put her back in the tank; she survived and had her babies. As far as communicating this experience, this guppy wasn't talking much. I would have years to wait until experiencing the possibility of animal communication.

Once, in a fleeting conversation, I learned that my older brother had had a black cocker spaniel as a pet. While out walking, the spaniel broke free from his leash and ran off. He was never found. Perhaps this sad event left a permanent mark on my family. There were no pictures of him; he was never spoken of except for that momentary word, which my young ears did not miss. I paid the price for this; I was never allowed a pet. I lost out big time. I think of all the years of love and companionship I missed. But believe me, I have done my best to make up for lost time. Everything that walks, hops, swims, and flies has found a haven in my home over the years.

I rescue the misfits—the elderly, the ill, the emotionally troubled ones that others toss away. I have literally found treasures tied up in garbage bags, left alongside the busy highway. Their stories will be told later.

I will attempt to keep my journey here in chronological order, but you must forgive me if I sometimes venture off the path. My mind writes as it thinks, always busy and energy-filled. This is my first attempt at writing some sort of memoir. I hope you enjoy the journey and its sidetracks along with me.

I never felt part of the 'normal pack' in society. I have strayed from the accepted route, the seen path, and sidetracked onto unseen territories and energies. Perhaps this book will cast a bit of sunlight on that path for those afraid of paths not trod by the normal pack, as well.

- Two -
You Can't Run Away from Fate

I was very sheltered as a child. I was driven to and from school, even though it was on the next block. I made several attempts at walking, but I remember a couple of frightening experiences when dogs would run after me and chase me all the way home. I would barely make it in the house. This fear of the unknown was tempered by a deep curiosity about these beings. I guess they had stuff to tell me back then; I just wasn't ready to listen yet.

I once opened the door to my home and had a cat race into the basement. I screamed so loudly that I don't know which of us was more startled. My father spent the evening searching every corner and closet of the basement; he was certain she came in to have a litter of kittens. She didn't come in to have kittens. Perhaps she was just stepping in for a chat. She recognized a kindred soul, even though I hadn't yet.

Years later, as I teenager, I tried to smuggle kittens into the house. I could never keep them. Even though I felt ashamed to bring them back to the owners, saying my family would not allow me to have them, I never tossed them outside. I am proud of the fact that I always returned them, in spite of my embarrassment, so they would be safe. I think that caring is a part of who we are. Some can toss a life by the side of the road, or in a garbage bag, and not look back. Others cannot look away.

My brother especially vetoed my attempts to bring in any feline guests. I have to laugh now; he has a house full of cats. His car trunk is never without a bag of cat food should a stray happen across his path.

My intuitive and telepathic experiences as a child were kept well hidden by me. Or so I thought. It wasn't until years later, after the death of my mother, that an aunt told me how she knew all along.

Even as a kid, I lived on an "enchanted block." We were known as the street of thousands of starlings that would visit at dusk, stay the night, and wreak havoc on our ears, lawns, and peace. The trees would shift into black masses of fluttering wings; the skies would blacken. Thousands would roost in our trees. Mornings would bring the casualty tolls of those involved in nighttime fights. To me, Alfred Hitchcock's horror film *The Birds* is the scariest picture of all time. I knew these things could happen; my childhood lived through them.

So, you might say I have been influenced and affected by animals all of my life. I just didn't realize the true extent until much later.

- Three -
Wolf at My Door

Thirty some years ago, I met an animal spirit that walked this earth unlike any I have since encountered in my years as an Animal Communicator and Reiki Master.

I lived in a rural area of woods and farmlands in a modern complex built next to rambling cornfields and potato fields. I would spend my days alone here. My husband traveled a lot with his job, and I was still the "quiet child" who found socializing and finding friends difficult. My furry companion was a little Persian kitten, my first acquisition as a newlywed.

One day, I spotted him.

He would come out of the woods and walk around the complex. I must have been insane, but I opened the door and let him in…

LET HIM IN…I think back, and knowing now what I do about animals and behaviors, I totally believe it was fearless innocence, or destiny, or both, that caused me to open my door to the power of something that could have killed my helpless little kitten or me.

But he didn't. I fed him, and he left.

He returned the next day—and the following one, too. I don't remember the day I decided, but one day, I let him in to stay.

Now, I had told my parents I found a stray puppy and was feeding him. The day I decided to "keep" him, I called my husband and told him I let a puppy in the home. He hadn't known about our daily visits. I told him he was a German shepherd. My husband had been raised with shepherds, so he was not against this proposal. You can imagine his surprise when my husband came home from work that evening and entered our apartment expecting to find a little puppy and encountering 100+ lbs. of sheer muscle instead.

But he won over my husband. He sat patiently as my husband picked off the countless ticks embedded in his fur.

What was he? No one really knew. The vet did not know for certain, but I could tell the vet was afraid of him. I had to hold onto him during a visit for a bronchial infection that he developed from living in the wild. When I walked him, people would whisper among themselves about what he was….a police guard dog perhaps? He looked like a furry shepherd, but he had beautiful golden yellow eyes—the eyes of a wolf. How I managed to control him on a leash is a mystery to me. He had the power to send me reeling with one lunge.

He was strong, all muscle. And he had no tail. The vet couldn't tell me if he had ever had one.

Everyone feared him, but he was my guardian. I truly believe that he looked upon me as his mate and my home as his den. But therein was the problem…

He had to be free. He would leave the apartment and disappear for the day. I knew he had to go hunt, to be free, and he would return to my den at night.

Neighbors in the complex did not like this. He was very fearsome looking, and they were afraid of his roaming around. I would take him with me to the laundry complex and feel like I was completely protected. No one dared approach us.

He was well fed at home, but he just couldn't bear a life of being closed in. The minute I opened the door…let me rephrase that…the minute I even contemplated walking over to open the door, his 100 lbs of power would be there, wrestling my body for room to break free. He would never hurt me. He never once growled at me. He just smushed his whole body against the tiniest opening to the wilderness and ran out.

Things progressed to the point that I would have to lock him in the bedroom before I went out. If I was coming home and he wasn't locked in, the minute I opened the door, he was gone like a bolt of pure lightning. We started getting complaints from the neighbors, and I could understand why. Many of them would be walking their little toy terriers or poodles, and I admit—this wolf looked bad, very bad. All he wanted was his freedom. But he would always come home to me. I would go to the store, and he would emerge out of the woods and follow my car down the road for a ways. It was just like the scene from *Dancing with Wolves*, when Two Socks follows Kevin Costner's character. I would watch him darting along my car in the complex, so afraid that he would be run over, and then see him running along the woods tracking my car. He would keep this up until I got on the main road and then disappear into the woods, only to return to my doorstep when I arrived home again. My brother called him the "Omen." He would be standing guard at my door like a sentry protecting his den. My family was witness to all of these occurrences. As I said, there will never be another like him.

Things progressed for the worse. He never once did any harm to me, my cat Smokey, or the toy poodle I would later bring into my home. In fact, I have pictures of Peanut Buttercup sleeping on him. He could have easily devoured her in one bite.

The only time he ever unknowingly could have hurt me was when he jumped up at me. He liked to jump when he was happy, and since I was only about 100 lbs. myself, he knocked me backwards and down against the wall.

My husband was different. Jealousy was escalating; it seems the dog was starting to view me more and more as his mate and was harboring increasing resentment about sharing me with another. He would sleep at night under my bed and start growling when my husband came into the bedroom.

When I tell you this dog—wolf?—was frightening, imagine hearing that growl coming for you…

That is when it got to a point when my husband could not deal with it anymore. He took the dog for a drive down the road and let him go free one night. It was a terribly rainy night; when my husband opened the door to leave for work the next morning, you guessed it—in walked a wet wolf home to his den. My husband was so impressed that the dog had tracked his way home that he was given a reprieve. But not for long.

Neighbors' complaints escalated. Jealousy toward my husband escalated. I always tried to take the dog with me. Once, I remember going shopping and trying to get out of the car without him and catching his paw in the door. He wasn't hurt, luckily; I was more traumatized than he.

We were in danger of being evicted from the complex, and things at home were becoming dangerous for the "two mates" in my life. My husband took the dog for a long, long drive into the woods very far from home.

I was heart-broken. I went back home to my parents for a couple of days.

My parents drove me back to my apartment. It was early afternoon in the dead of winter. I remember my mother turning to my dad and saying, "Let's go. Don't you see she has her hat on? She is going out looking." And she was right.

I took off in my little, used Vega. Those of you old enough to remember the Vega will commiserate when I say it wasn't the best of vehicles (although it always got me where I wanted to go). I drove for about an hour to a densely wooded area. I searched and searched into the woods alongside the road and saw nothing.

Keep in mind that I was a petite, young girl of 21 or 22 years of age, alone in these woods. The world seemed "safer" then.

In desperation, I drove back out to the main road, found a public pay phone, and called my mom. Their drive took about 1 ½ hours, and they had reached home by now. I cried and told her I couldn't find him. It was getting dark, it was cold, and I was getting scared of being so far away from home by myself.

What do you think my mother said? "Get home immediately. What's wrong with you?"?

No. My mother said, "Go back."

I couldn't believe my ears. I was crying and tired and had lost all hope, and my mother was telling me to go back.

I went back.

Maybe my mother knew more about me than I realized. Maybe she knew things about herself she never told me. But I drove back through those woods in the diminishing light of late afternoon and came to a clearing that went far back until it met a line of trees deepening into the woods far from the road.

I remembered the days I spent by myself as a child, sending thoughts to people, transmitting energetic ideas. And a light went off inside me. If I could do it with people, then maybe I could do it with animals.

I stood there outside my car, and I "talked" to him.

Time passed, and I continued...

From the distance, I could make out a tiny speck. My heart pounded. Was this a deer, or could this be him?

I yelled out his name and saw the form turn towards me......and start to RUN.

Now remember, I told you he loved to jump. I watched this being gaining force and momentum for a distance, like a missile aimed directly at me. But he didn't knock me down.

We got in my tiny Vega. I had never driven so long with him in the car, but he was no trouble. I took him home.

The happiness didn't last long...problems recurred. Finally, my husband took him hours away to a shelter. After relentless begging, he told me where he had taken him.

My family, seeing my distress, agreed to take the dog back to their home. My brother drove me hours away to an animal shelter out by Ft. Dix in New Jersey. When I got there, I asked where he was. They showed me some animals, but none were him.

My heart was sinking...but then, one of the shelter workers said, "You don't mean this one, do you?" The worker led me to a back room where, docile in his cage, sat my boy. I say docile because I know the workers had drugged him. There was no spark of knowing me in his eyes; he was drugged into submission, probably hours from being killed. The shelter workers could not believe I was taking this "thing" back with me. I remember them asking for payment for a being they were going to destroy momentarily. To me, he was priceless. We paid and left without saying another word.

We took him to my parents' home. I was so very worried he would "wake up" mid-trip, but it seemed the grace of God was always with us, and we made it home without incident. Ft. Dix was a long, long trip from my parents' home.

It was there he spent the following months of his life, in my parents' basement. He ate some wooden chair legs. He loved having my mom vacuum him; he would lie down on his back and let her literally vacuum his fur. My parents joked that I came to visit *him*, not *them*. He could recognize my voice across the room through the telephone receiver. We would "talk" regularly; they joked that I called him, not them, as well.

Once, my mom tied him on a chain in the yard and found him hanging in mid-air, trying to jump over the fence. To this day, I still don't know how she managed to get him down. Another time, she found him with a kitten in his mouth. Luckily, he let it go, and the kitten, still alive, walked away. But as I mentioned earlier, never once did he so much as scratch my little toy poodle or cat. He seemed to sense they were part of my pack. He could have devoured them easily.

He was well fed and cared for, kept in the cleanest of conditions with a little room to roam around, but he was lost without his woods. He had to be kept on a very long, heavy chain so he wouldn't bolt out the door each time it was opened. Was this a happy life? I knew, no matter how well-kept he was, he longed to be free again.

My father was afraid to walk him. This dog was too powerful even for my 250 lb. dad. Once, he got away, and my father had to race after him to catch him. One of my father's best friends died from a heart attack after chasing his dog; I know that fear plagued my dad.

One day, my mother told me on the phone that the dog was gone.

My dad, a police captain, had taken him to the facility that trains police dogs and asked them to try to "break" his wildness. My parents didn't tell me they were doing this. The facility told my dad, "He is a killer. We cannot break him." My dad left him there, never asking what they did with him. I don't know…maybe that is best.

To this day, I wonder if I should have left him in the woods. My life changed the day a wolf came out of the woods to my door…or maybe it changed the day I went into the woods myself.

By the way, his name was Snoopy—not your typical "killer" name. He wasn't a killer to me; he was my friend. Whether I should have left him in the woods is a question that has haunted me, but people were complaining about him and, eventually, I think he would have been killed by animal control if left to wander.

He liked to live in two worlds—the world of human companionship and the world of the wild wolf. I, myself, have turned out to be much the same, living in both the "normal" and metaphysical world. I work as a Reiki Master and Animal Intuitive and firmly believe that one day, his spirit will join mine again. I now devote my life to the rescue and care of the "misfits."

I know that some can never be saved. Those beings will usually be sent to the Rainbow Bridge, hopefully with love and light surrounding them. One day, they will be waiting for me and all the devoted, tireless animal rescuers who carry the burden of grief within their hearts for those lost without knowing love and compassion on earth.

I know in my heart that my Snoopy waits for me in a beautiful place where he can roam between his two worlds.

- Four -
The Energy that Lingers After Death

I have a farmhouse in Gettysburg, Pennsylvania, a place thought by many to be America's most haunted land.

I have always believed in the paranormal. I saw my first apparition at the age of about eight.

It wasn't a dream. How many of your childhood dreams do you remember? Remember so vividly that your head and heart can transport back there in an instant, filling your senses as though time had stood still?

I can do this...

In the middle of the night, I woke with the feeling of not being alone in my bedroom. I looked up to see a hazy, grey face...just a head, suspended in air, looking down at me...

It was an old face. I was very frightened. I didn't scream; I think I was too terrified to utter a sound.

In my childhood mind, I thought whoever or whatever this was was there to take me away...take me back with him or her...

So, I closed my eyes, slid under the covers, and pretended to be asleep. If this *thing* thought I was asleep, it wouldn't harm me. It would leave. This made perfect sense in my eight-year-old brain.

I remember breaking out into a cold sweat...

I always remember the cold sweat. When a person says he or she broke out in a cold sweat, I understand. I understand how you can be freezing and shivering, but sweating at the same time.

I stayed this way, concealed against doom under the blankets, for what seemed like an eternity (although the adult mind in me now knows this is untrue).

Then, I felt the knowing sensation that whoever or whatever this was, was leaving. I could feel the distance between us growing...

It is hard to explain this to someone who has not experienced it. I can only make a feeble attempt.

Then, I heard what I can only describe as the most beautiful, haunting music I have ever heard. I cannot replicate it in my memory. I can only replicate the feeling of intense beauty that I felt.

To me, this was the music of the Angels and Heaven...

I never shared my experience with anyone—not my parents, no one. I somehow don't think they would have believed me. But Fate has its way of catching up to you, and the Paranormal once again came knocking on my door.

In later years, I came to realize my mother knew much more about what was going on with me than I ever realized. I wish I had shared this with her. It was a huge burden for an eight year old to keep inside.

This leads up to my first experience with animals and the afterlife. So many times, I have been asked if I believe animals continue to exist in another dimension, waiting for us. I genuinely believe they do. I have had several extraordinary occurrences that tell me such.

- Five -
Do Pets Possess Souls That Live On?

Working as a Reiki Master and Animal Intuitive Communicator has brought the same question repeatedly upon me: Do our pets go to Heaven? I genuinely believe the energy of our pets lives on. It is energy of pure love, and I have been privileged to feel this energy and offer comfort to many grieving pet owners.

It was my first toy poodle, Peanut Buttercup, who taught me that dogs do live on. Peanuts was my first child. Before Snoopy came to my door, I had spotted this little ball of fur in a pet shop cage. (I was extremely naïve; none of us knew about puppy mills back then.)

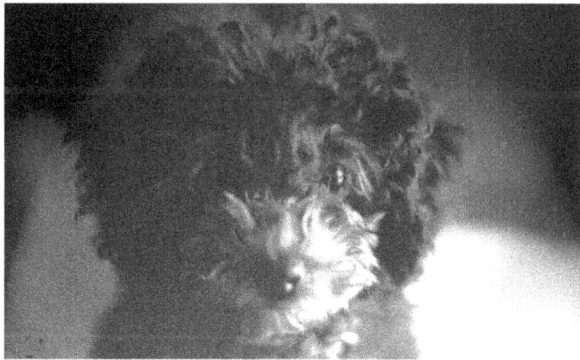

I had scrimped and saved my food budget money for weeks, eating more Kraft Macaroni and Cheese than I care to remember, all for the purpose of bringing her home. Then Snoopy came.

"I still want her." I had a bargain with my husband; if I could save the money, I could get her. He had to agree.

So, Peanuts came home.

Peanuts was a true puppy mill example. She was plagued with seizures right from the start. And she was obsessed with playing catch. Not with balls, not with toys, but with rocks.

Peanuts loved to chew rocks; when a tennis ball was not readily available, the nearest rock would do. She would chew it and repeat the process until exhaustion. Nothing we did could stop her. She loved rocks.

Peanuts loved me, too. When I had my first child, Peanuts stood at the top of the hallway steps at my mom's house for three days, waiting for me. She was my baby. Now, she had to learn to play second fiddle to another. This was very hard for her. She never really liked being tousled by small fingers.

Once, when she was a baby, we left Peanuts and my cat Smokey home to go to the movies. We had a sliding glass door with a floor-length curtain. Upon our return, my cat was waiting at the door, talking up a storm. She was the feline equivalent of Lassie at the well. Looking in the room, we saw Peanuts dangling. She had chewed a hole in the curtain, put her head through, and was literally hanging on for dear life. I cringe to think of what would have happened if we had not come home in time.

Thankfully, Peanuts lived to be twelve years old. However, she grew very thin towards the end. We took her to the vet, and she endured countless tests. The vet decided it was her teeth, and she underwent painful surgery. I'll never forget the ride home; she cried so mournfully in my lap. I have never heard cries such as this again in my life.

The surgery made no difference. Peanuts' teeth were in bad shape from chewing rocks, but something far worse was making my little girl so frail.

Looking back, with the expertise that can only come from owning a menagerie, I realize some sort of cancer must have been invading her tiny body—perhaps liver or kidney. She had good days and bad ones. We treasured the good ones.

Then it was my son's birthday. He wasn't in school yet, and his favorite treat was to go for fast food fries. The day after his birthday, Peanuts seemed okay. It was a nice, cool spring day. I parked in the shade and took him inside the restaurant for fries. We didn't stay long; he brought his fries back to the car and shared some with Peanuts.

On the way home, we passed by our neighborhood cemetery to visit my aunt's grave. Her headstone was only about three in from the road. My son and I parked under a big shade tree in front, got out, and walked to the stone and back to the car in under 2 minutes. We often visited and took care of my aunt's resting place.

When I got back to the car, I got annoyed that Peanuts had sprawled herself across the driver's seat and wouldn't move. Then I realized she wasn't alive. In that space of minutes, she had died. How, I don't know. Perhaps a massive heart attack. But I will always be sorry I raised my voice for her to move.

I told my son she was sleeping. I forced myself to keep my composure and drove to my mom's home. I left my son, went home, took care of Peanuts, and sat down and mourned for my little girl.

I remember crying alone in my kitchen, head bowed in my arms on the table, when I heard a voice in my head. It was not like hearing words; it was like hearing thoughts. I heard my aunt say, in a gruff manner, "Why are you crying? I have her, and I will take care of her as you take care of me."

Almost instantly, a feeling of peace flooded over me.

I confided this to my mother. She said that gruffness was my aunt's "way" when she was annoyed at something.

Then she shared a secret with me.

My aunt had one mentally challenged son. Her husband had passed many years before. My mother and she would visit his grave. My aunt would often tell her, "You have children. They will look after your stone. I have no one, no one to care about where I lay."

So my aunt was telling me *Thank you*. Thank you for caring for me; now I will care for her. My aunt loved animals, especially birds. I know Peanuts was in good hands.

Not too long after, my mother would join her sister and my little silver poodle. Decades later, on that same day, the day after my son's birthday, my father would join them.

That big cemetery tree was cut down; when I stop and park to visit my parents and my aunt, I remember a little silver poodle, too. Just like the tree, she is not here, but her presence is remembered.

- Six -
Do Dogs See Spirits?

I can say, rather unequivocally, that our pets do see spirits.

I have a dog now, a Pomeranian, very attuned to who is passing through my house. There have been days when he refuses to go sleep in his favorite spot upstairs at night. When the atmosphere has cleared, he once again revisits.

When I adopted him from a friend, I mentioned this to her. She smiled and said, "Boy, was he ever meant to go to you! We have known this all along; we were just waiting for you to say something."

My Reiki office was housed in a newly-renovated but very old building. There were spirits there. It had been a physician's office. There must have been very ill patients making a last visit during a century past.

Many dogs reacted to the energy in my office, always in a certain corner of the room. In the Paranormal field, there are certain energy vortexes that serve as doorways between dimensions. These sensitive animals always felt the doorway.

After Peanuts died, I got another silver poodle named Skippy. My mother loved Skippy. She got to know him before she passed away. She never rang my bell; instead, she always yelled "Skippy" at my front door, and he would bark.

One night, not long after my mother passed away, I was alone downstairs late in the evening. My husband was not home; my young children were asleep.

I was in my kitchen, which seems to hold the vortex doorway in my house. I was standing at the sink, washing dishes. (Water is an excellent conduit for spirits. Most of our haunted towns are surrounded by water.)

I heard my mother yell, "Skippy." Skippy heard it, too. I was very frightened; I wouldn't open the door. For years—decades even—this haunted me. I spoke to another medium about this, and she allayed my sorrows. *Your mother didn't want you to answer; she just wanted you to hear her hello. Skippy heard it, too.* I saw his head turn around and heard his bark. He answered her.

This would not be the last time Skippy connected me to the Spirit Realm.

- Seven -
Skippy's Story

There are certain dogs in life known as "angel dogs." These are the ones that grab onto your heart with a climber's grappling hook and dig into the very depths.

Skippy Francis was one of those dogs…a shadow in the guise of a tiny, silver toy poodle.

We would go walking in the park together. He didn't need a leash for he never strayed; the Ritz Bits I kept in my pocket were much too alluring. Even without the Ritz Bits, Skippy would remain by my side. That is the kind of friend he was—loyal through and through.

The day we found him, he picked me out. I knelt down, and this little ball of fur started pulling on my sneaker laces, untying them. He was good at laces…he sure tied my heartstrings.

Peanuts had suffered so badly from seizures, but the breeder explicitly promised that Skippy had no predisposition to them. That was true for the first six months. Then my little boy suffered from them for the rest of his twelve years. At the end, he had congestive heart failure and was blind, but still his love was unwavering.

One spring, my husband asked what I wanted for Mother's Day. In some homes, women ask for jewelry or clothing. I always ask for little balls of fur. Besides my children, Skippy was my best Mother's Day present.

That same year, at Christmastime, my husband made the mistake of asking what I wanted. Skippy got a brother that Christmas, a little toy silver poodle named Peter Pan. We called him Petey for short.

Skippy and Peter Pan—I think you see where this is going.

Skippy didn't want a brother at first. I remember he took dozens of trips upstairs, carrying each of his toys one by one. I had a loveseat that rested against the railing. One by one, Skippy tossed those toys at my head, his mark of displeasure that I had brought this little vagrant in to share his space.

Soon, however, they made peace, and the two brothers remained friends through life. Skippy passed about a year or two before Petey.

The day Skippy passed, I was listening to a beautiful song by Andrea Bocelli. If you have never heard it, I recommend you seek out its haunting melody and lyric. It is entitled, "Go Where Love Goes."

I knew my Skippy was not well. To entice his appetite, I made a chicken soup and selected the tender meat for him to enjoy. I persuaded him to take only a couple of bites.

While I was listening to this song, Skippy walked into the room and looked up at me with a gaze in his eyes that told me he would be leaving soon. Tears filled my eyes, and I started singing him the poignant lyrics, telling him to "go where love goes."

My beautiful little boy died in my arms that night. I believe he did go with love, and he is waiting there for me one day to join him.

Skippy did visit me one last time to say hello…

Here is the story of Skippy's return visit from Heaven:

A Visit from a Canine Angel in Heaven

Many, many years ago, I had a little toy poodle, or I should say, I had a little shadow.

He followed me everywhere.

Skippy was one of those special dogs. Many dogs fill the pages of my life, but sometimes, one comes along that is a "highlighted word" amongst those pages.

Skippy was that highlight.

He picked me out. When I met him, he grabbed hold of my sneaker laces, tugged, and untied them…and tied my heartstrings from that moment on.

Skippy lived to be twelve. He suffered from seizures as the years passed and died of heart failure.

But his heart didn't die.

Some time after his passing, the UPS delivery man rang my bell. As I opened the door to answer, my neighbor from across the street came running over in a frantic state.

We had only exchanged short pleasantries prior to this; I didn't know him very well, so this was surprising.

He said, "Your little dog…he was outside on your front lawn, and then I saw him run up the street. I know you don't keep him outside. I was worried that he got out by accident."

I told him he was mistaken, that this wasn't my dog, but he kept insisting it was. I didn't want to tell him Skippy had passed away, so I just smiled and politely repeated, "No, it's not my dog." Even the UPS man was bewildered by the persistence of this man.

My neighbor didn't know the work I do, but many years later, when his elderly dog became very ill, he came to me—by chance or not so much by chance—and I treated his beloved dog with Reiki. Their veterinarian said his beloved dog would be gone in months. He instead lived a couple of years. I grew to love him as if he were my own. My neighbor became a firm believer in Reiki, and our families have become good friends.

After his beloved husky crossed, I told him the story of my Skippy, and I told him what he had seen.

He had seen my Skippy coming to visit.

Skippy didn't make his presence known to my eyes, but he sent a calling card to a neighbor. Even dogs have a sense of humor. What better messenger for a heavenly visit than the UPS man?

Look for messages—you never know who might deliver them. I know my Skippy came to call that afternoon, if only to say, "Hi, Mom, I'm still around." He thought it appropriate for the UPS man to be in on the delivery, too. He was the best present ever delivered to my door.

Our pets remain with us. They walk by our sides, and their shadows remain. Death does not untie our bonds of love.

- Eight -
Peter Pan

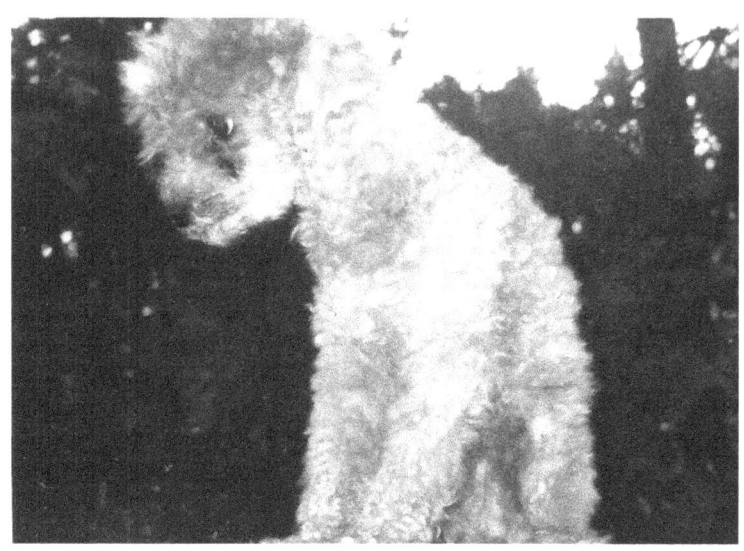

Peter Pan was the third silver toy poodle to become part of my home and heart, half-brother to Skippy and bane of his existence at first.

Peter was born on October 12th. I thought about naming him Columbo after the popular TV series character of the time, but I chose Peter Pan instead. (Not so off-base, since Peter Falk played Columbo.)

Petey, as he became known, was the quintessential Peter Pan. He loved to play, he loved attention, and he loved to be held. He never lost his puppy zeal for running around. He stayed skinny, with the metabolism of a hummingbird (and about the same speed as he dashed across the yard).

His youthful zest for life served him well. Petey was almost killed in a dog attack. He was rushed to an emergency facility and placed in an oxygen chamber. It was touch-and-go for several days, but Petey came home.

The vet warned me that his personality might change after such trauma. Not my Petey. The same lively, never-grow-old boy came bandaged through my door.

Petey will live on as my happy little boy, never growing old except in physical years, much like his namesake. He never wanted to *grow up*...

I am glad his youthful puppy legs once raced to greet me every day for twelve years.

- Nine -
Reiki Finds Me

A close friend introduced me to Reiki. I had always been a pretty energetic being myself, helped along by a narrow scrape with electricity when I was a young adult.

I think this close encounter left me extremely sensitive to energy around me. I can read auras and have given medical intuitive sessions to guide where there is energy disruption in the system.

My friend's babbling on about this wonderful energy intrigued me. I looked up the name of a local Reiki Master and enrolled myself in a Reiki I workshop.

I have to admit, I was leery. During the first half of the workshop, the teacher even noticed my vague disinterest.

Then came the attunement. It was as if a switch turned on inside my brain. My teacher noticed; she said there was a complete turnaround from the person who walked through the door that morning.

I continued on to the next level and then to the final level of Reiki Master. My teacher said Reiki finds you; you only think you find it. Perhaps this is true. For it was meant to find me.

I wanted to combine my love for animals with Reiki, so my friend (who had introduced me to Reiki) and I opened a Reiki practice. She was to concentrate on people; I would focus on the care of animals. Soon after, she decided this was not her path and left the practice.

That is how I began sessions on both people and animals.

I have met some wonderful people and have shared extraordinary experiences through Reiki. In the following chapters, I would like to honor a few memorable beings who shared their last days of life with me. It has been my privilege to guide them to the Bridge.

It has been a joy to see the suffering of some beings lightened through Reiki. I never promised miracles or cures, but so many pet owners told me that they saw improvement in the way their pets walked or lived life after our sessions. And most importantly of all, Reiki offers peace and comfort at the time of transition. Pet owners would come back and thank me, saying their veterinarians remarked how peacefully their pets had crossed.

Each one I shared Reiki with became a friend. The friendship was always bittersweet for the ones who chose to cross. But I would not have missed our moments together to spare my heart the ache of their leaving.

- Ten -
Gretchen

When I opened my office, the first pet to come to me was Gretchen, a furry Angel.

My daughter was with me in the office as we looked down from the upstairs window. My office was on the second floor. Out of the car parked in front of the building emerged a woman holding a large German shepherd.

My daughter exclaimed, "I knew it was going to be a shepherd."

I witnessed true devotion in action as this woman, not much larger than I, carried her shepherd up the flight of stairs to my office.

Gretchen suffered from a neurological disease which was leaving her immobilized in her hind legs. Coincidentally (or not coincidentally if you believe in the Universe's Intentions), I had lost a German shepherd girl to a similar disease not much long beforehand. My Cinnamon Girl lived to be twelve years old. We constructed a ramp for her to use during her last months.

I had never euthanized a pet before. When the task of getting up became impossible for her, I gave in to one of life's hardest decisions. I called the vet in the morning. My husband laid a blanket in the back of his truck, and I went in to say farewell to my girl. I told her if she wanted to stay to let me know, and I would not take her.

I left the room and continued getting ready, though I don't know how one ever gets ready for a journey like this. My husband came in to pick her up. My Cinnamon Girl was standing—yes, she had walked to the doorway and was looking at me.

"I am not taking her," I said.

My husband responded that if I wasn't taking her, then I would have to call the vet and cancel.

I called the vet. Cinnamon told me her decision, and I kept my promise to her.

For a few more months, we took care of her. We still had to lift her up to go outside, and the final days were difficult, but she passed away at home with all of us around her. That was her decision. Ask, and LISTEN to your pet; he or she will tell you.

So, Gretchen had a place in my heart before I even laid a hand on her with Reiki. Gretchen came back to my office weekly for Reiki. Her owner saw improvement in her walking, sometimes even before she left my office.

Gretchen was my Angel in more than one way. She helped me support the office when clients were few and far between, and I will always be grateful to her mom for providing funding for me to continue.

Gretchen would talk to me during her Reiki sessions.

Pets communicate in pictures. Receiving them is like placing a puzzle together, and interpreting them can be a challenge sometimes. (This is a two-way street. Animals speak to us every single day, and we speak to them constantly without saying a word. They interpret the pictures in our minds. When our minds are filled with fear, we send them fear. When our hearts are filled with sadness, they take on our burdens. When our souls unite in loving bonds, those bonds are impenetrable.)

Gretchen showed me a scene of her owner and herself at a gravesite. I told her owner, but she said this made no sense; she and Gretchen didn't do this.

Her abrupt answer silenced my words and confidence. I did not publicly work as an Animal Communicator at this time; I still had not found the confidence to share this with my clients. I left it at that, but it always haunted me. There was a reason this dog was placing such importance on this image.

Months went by, and Gretchen's quality of life far exceeded veterinary expectations. However, she started to decline in the autumn.

One day, during an office visit with me, she sent me a beautiful image of playing in the autumn leaves. Still not confident, maybe more so after the last rejection of communication, I kept silent. As Gretchen and her owner were leaving, her mom stopped at the door and paused. She said the weekend had been an especially beautiful one. She said she had carried Gretchen out onto a huge pile of leaves, one of her favorite play activities, and let her enjoy the day with her. I kept quiet. I never wanted people to think I had taken advantage of shared information. Those that know my work today know I do most of my Intuitive Sessions with no information given except names. I still am haunted by my silence. How much of a difference could I have made if I had told her mom? Part of me hopes these words find her today.

In my animal communication workshops, I now stress one of the most important aspects—CONFIDENCE.

Come Christmas, Gretchen's mom had to fly to Florida to visit family. Gretchen was to stay with a trusted friend. I was honored she gave her friend my number in case something happened while she was away. It was right after the holidays that I received the call. Gretchen was in trouble—might I come over? Her mom was catching the soonest flight home.

I felt so privileged to stay with Gretchen. Her friend told me that Gretchen only acted a certain way with special, beloved people. He said she acted that way when I came in the door. I sat with her, gave her Reiki, and told her to hang on for her mom.

Reiki is a wonderful source of comfort to those nearing transition. Gretchen hung on; her mom came home, and Gretchen transitioned at the vet's peacefully the next day.

After she passed, her mom wrote me a beautiful letter, which I framed and kept. It has their pictures on it. They will always be important to me.

And one final thing...Gretchen's mom spoke with me some time later. She had been a young widow. Filled with grief, perhaps anger, she said she never once visited her husband's grave. After Gretchen's passing, she did. This loving dog saw the hurt inside her owner's heart and sought to set it free...through pictures to me.

- Eleven -
The Priceless Look on a Vet's Face

Life's accomplishments and pride come to us at unexpected times. One memorable moment for me was when I convinced a veterinarian that there was *something* to Animal Communication.

She came to my office holding a shaking, nervous ball of fear. A puppy mill survivor, a little Papillon named Lucy.

Reiki helped calm Lucy; instead of cowering in the corner, she sat huddled under the safety of my office chair—a little breakthrough. But it was the Animal Communication sessions that amazed her owner.

"If Lucy can communicate, perhaps she can show you her favorite treat."

I looked at the vet and said, "Hot dogs."

Hot dogs??? Would a vet be giving hot dogs as a treat?

Remember…CONFIDENCE.

I looked at the vet and saw her lower jaw extend several feet toward the office carpet. With eyes that revealed shock and amazement, she said, "I buy those little baby jar hot dogs. They are Lucy's favorite treat."

I smiled.

As I continued the session, I told her that Lucy was showing me a blue elephant.

I asked, "Does she play with this, or is it in your house?"

Thinking about it, she responded, "No, wait...there is a statue, but it isn't blue......perhaps..."

"No," I insisted, "the BLUE ELEPHANT...." It wasn't until after the session ended that the image I relayed was validated.

Lucy and her owner had just left the office. Minutes later, I heard someone running up my stairs. The out-of-breath vet said, "I take Lucy to work with me. She stays in a crate in my office. Dangling in the crate is a toy. It's an elephant...I THINK IT'S BLUE...She doesn't like anyone going near that toy."

I smiled again.

The vet wrote this to me:

"I was absolutely amazed at the connection Shirl was able to make with my dog, Lucy. Lucy is a 13-year-old Papillon and a former puppy mill breeder dog. She is not very well socialized and extremely skittish. But by the second visit, Lucy came out from under the chair and rested comfortably out in the open. Shirl was able to let me know certain things that Lucy communicated that were so specific, it was surreal. I truly appreciate this gift that Shirl has and the gift she gave me with the insight into Lucy. I recommend that everyone should let his or her pets meet Shirl."

- Twelve -
Cats Like Reiki—and Birds, Too

Cats love Reiki. They just walk in the room with an attitude like, "At last, someone finally gets it." They accept the Reiki almost instantly. Dogs are a little more wary; they have to take some time to sniff around, investigate this energy, before settling down for a peaceful session.

At my office, I had the privilege of meeting quite a remarkable little cat named Cocoa. He was so thin and frail when he came to see me. I gave him Reiki; he let me maneuver his little body in any position I chose. He was a pure delight; I fell in love with him. I knew his time was near, but there are some things I wish to keep silent and not tell the owner.

Soon after, his owner came to talk to me. The door had been left open; Cocoa had gone out, something which he never did. They couldn't find him. He never came home. I knew this remarkable being wanted to spare his family his final moments and chose to wander off by himself to cross.

Birds know Reiki, too. I once had a very sick little parrot come sit on my shoulder. Normally, she wasn't that loving, but on this particular morning, she didn't want to leave.

I could feel her whole energy aura. The aura feels differently close to death. It is a hard feeling to describe. It is as if the energy of the physical body is melding with the energy of the Universe. I felt this in her. Later that afternoon, I found her head down in her water tray.

I now understand why she didn't want to leave my shoulder. She was saying good-bye.

- Thirteen -
Dakota

I saw Dakota for years. He was a handsome husky that lived across the street. I exchanged only the pleasantries of a waving hand with his owners. My closest encounter was that day I wrote about earlier when the UPS man came to my door.

Yes, Dakota's dad was that neighbor. He still didn't know of my work as a Reiki Master, or that I had a Reiki practice in town. But the Universe picks the right moments to share needed information and opens doorways for each of us to walk through when the time is right.

The right time came when Dakota became extremely ill.

My husband was outside doing yard work. My distraught neighbor shared his anguish over a beloved pet's dismal prognosis.

"You know, my wife Shirl sees pets at her Reiki practice."

"Reiki, what is that?" he asked.

And that is how it began, our journey together.

This sweet dog, given only a short time to journey, surpassed all the odds laid out by his veterinarian, living with good quality of life and joy for much longer than his time allotment diagnosis. I was there with him on his journey, right until the final day when he lay stretched out in the sun on my neighbor's lawn.

Here is Dakota's story, in the words of my neighbor and now friend:

Shirl,

As promised, here is my testimonial. You will recall late last spring that Dakota was diagnosed with acute kidney failure. The vet administered a form of dialysis by intravenous on 2 or 3 occasions, each time only slightly reducing his BUN kidney values. He was also on several medications. He lost over 20 pounds, about 20% of his body weight, had multiple bouts of diarrhea and vomiting, and had no appetite and no energy. The vet finally suggested we not put Dakota through any more treatments and indicated he might have a month or so to live.

We came to learn of the services you provide, and after speaking with you, you offered to practice Reiki treatments on him. All you ever promised was to attempt to get Dakota in a better frame of mind physically and mentally to better deal with the stress of his illness and, to whatever degree he had the ability to, fight off his illness.

Miraculously, after treating him for about a month, he began to regain his appetite, have more energy, and in general have a better quality of life. By the end of the summer, after visiting with the vet, we started to see his kidney values reduce, although not back to normal levels, low enough for Dakota to manage his illness. The vet indicated to us that she was amazed and had never had a dog with Dakota's condition make this kind of turn around. We indicated to her the services you were performing on Dakota, and she was quite impressed and simply told us to continue doing whatever we were doing.

It is now almost 10 months since Dakota became ill, and he is doing fine. We will continue to utilize your services to keep Dakota's frame of mind and stress level at a minimum to better allow him to continue fighting his own illness. This, along with some medication we are still giving him, has reduced his condition to some form of a manageable chronic illness.

We can't thank you enough for all you have done.

Respectfully and With Sincere Appreciation

Don't take the *time allotment* given by vets to heart; the Universe shall decide when that time has come. I have seen too many beloved pets continue on for much longer than medical expertise has predicted.

Combine that medical expertise with holistic and alternative therapies, and keep your pet's joy in life ignited. And above all, keep your joy ignited as well, for our pets know exactly what is kept in our hearts.

Tell them you accept and will be at peace when the Universe calls to them, when they know it is time to go. If an owner is at peace, the pet will be at peace, as well. I have seen many pets linger on because they see the grief and unwillingness to accept what must occur in their owners' eyes and hearts.

My dear friend Dakota left with peace. His owners will always miss him, but they opened their hearts to a new puppy. They named him Bandit because he stole their hearts.

Part Two

Embracing "Misfits"

- Fourteen -
Little Guy

Another example of a dog living past his *time allotment* was Little Guy. Little Guy was one of a kind; he can never be replaced. He was a pearl in a sea of oyster shells. I didn't know him the first thirteen or so years of his life, but that didn't stop him from singling me out as his new mom.

Prior to living with us, Little Guy had a loving mom. We learned that his previous owner was a very elderly woman who had passed away. Her family did not want him—he had *accidents* in the home—and they left him at a rescue in Pennsylvania.

I had lost a dog shortly before and went online to search for someone to ease my heartache. I found him; it was love at first sight. The minute I looked into his eyes, one misshapen with deformity and blindness, I knew he was the one. It was late August 2005 when I applied to the rescue. They voiced some apprehension—I had other dogs, and I was in New Jersey. This pairing of us was not going smoothly. I kept fighting; I wanted him so.

Finally, I resigned myself to look elsewhere and found a seven-month-old, runt-of-the-litter Pomeranian who had come out of rough beginnings. He was out in Ohio.

Then, Hurricane Katrina happened. Rescues were deluged with a flood of dogs left ownerless after the storm. They were being driven to shelters up North, one of them being the rescue that housed Little Guy. These circumstances softened the rules a bit. The shelter emailed and agreed to let me have Little Guy.

My husband drove one day out to Pennsylvania with me and one day out to Ohio, and we took them both. I have not one regret.

We picked up Little Guy on September 11, 2005. That anniversary was a tragic one. I had been close by when the Towers were bombed and watched the gaping holes, the flames, the death, and the disappearance into a pile of dust.

But now September 11th is a joyous day for me, as well. We made it Little Guy's new birthday.

Little Guy wasn't too well. They told me he had blackouts and would pass out due to an enlarged heart. He was blind in one eye, but he was a ball of energy. My whole family fell in love with him instantly. He walked in my door, jumped on my bed, and made my home his palace. He reigned in charge of all others; he ate first, he had his own stroller to take walks in, and he was my Prince.

Little Guy had a blackout a day or so after we brought him home. I remember so plainly crying over his still body, so worried my time with him would not be long.

Our vet examined him and said he might have a few weeks or a few months. He told us to enjoy all the moments we had, to just make him happy in his final days. We put him on several medications, and Little Guy, thankfully, ceased having those blackouts.

Little Guy lived six years longer. He had a couple of operations. He had twelve teeth pulled in the first one; six more were pulled during the second.

When I went away on vacation once, my children said Little Guy stayed in my bedroom the first couple of days and would not come downstairs. They had to bring his dinner up to him. We were so attached, as though we had been together all his thirteen years. It made no difference that I found him as an old man; he was loved as if I held him from a puppy.

The day I adopted him, I was holding him outside the rescue when a woman came up and asked, "How is your *little guy?*" His name was perfect. People just called him that, even before they knew it was really his name. She said we looked like we had been together his whole life, and that is how it felt.

Little Guy made it to his rescue's reunion picnic where, after six years, his former caregivers could not believe he was still alive. He enjoyed hot dogs, potato salad, and cake that afternoon, and he took home First Prize as the oldest dog there.

By now, though, his nineteen years were catching up with him.

Little Guy suffered a massive stroke not long afterwards. I fed him nourishment by eyedropper for eleven days, but then I had to make the hardest decision in all my years of loving animals. I euthanized Little Guy because my love could not bear his suffering anymore. I was with him; he went very peacefully. He left this world on the anniversary of my mother's death. If I searched the world over, no better mother could ever be found. If I searched this world for another Little Guy, no one could ever take his place, as well.

I would often worry that Little Guy would not remember me, that he would find his first mom at the Bridge and go back with her. I have come to understand that there is room for all moms and pets that are loved. He will find me one day again.

So, keep your heart open to as many days as life grants them to spend with you. Sometimes, a few weeks can turn into six loving years.

- Fifteen -
Greyfriars Bobby Blue

Bobby was brought home from Ohio the same week as Little Guy, a drive that amounted to five hours each way.

I named him after the famous Scotland terrier Greyfriars Bobby…and Blue because of his beautiful, blue eyes.

I am so glad I made that drive, for it was Fate that Bobby found a home with us. Frankly, I don't know what would have happened to my little boy if we had not made that trip.

Bobby was about seven months old. He had been the runt of the litter and was not expected to live. He had survived on a diet of cottage cheese; perhaps that nourishment inhibited full growth of his brain capacity. Bobby is dearly loved, but Bobby is a little challenged in the survival department.

Bobby had a type of seizure when he was little; to me, it was the equivalent of a canine form of autism. He would move to a corner, completely isolate himself from the world around, and just fade off into his own space. We put him on medication, but after a time, I weaned him off and the episodes naturally stopped. Sometimes, I think it was some type of behavior disassociation, the type exhibited by some orphans from foreign countries who lacked human bonding as babies.

Bobby also has stenosis of his ear canals. This benign narrowing is the cause of Bobby's frequent head tossing, just another one of his misfit attributes.

Bobby is very loved; in fact, he is spoiled rotten. He will not eat unless I hand feed him. His brain cells perk up considerably at the sound of the morning toaster, where he waits for his breakfast piece, and his ears can detect the treat bag from across the house. Not many teeth are left in Bobby's tiny mouth, but he manages to enjoy his toast and treats and hand feedings quite well.

Nothing gets Bobby's dander up. I once sucked up his tail in the vacuum, and he just stood there. Another time, I was changing the sofa slipcovers and saw a lump; Bobby was hidden under the covers not saying a word.

That is my Bobby—truly one-of-a-kind.

- Sixteen -
Anthony

In the pouring rain, a little Pomeranian stood very still alongside the entrance road to the Garden State Parkway. Cars whizzed past until my son came along...

That is how we "found" Anthony, named for the Patron Saint of *lost things*.....my Anthony, lost no more.

As I watched my son carry this tiny bundle in his arms, all I saw were these enormous eyes, whitened to the point of blindness.

He was so encrusted with mud and filth that we thought he was black in color. Then we saw them...the hundreds upon hundreds of fleas ingesting this helpless little being's blood.

I had never seen so many on a dog.

I called vets, I called groomers—no one wanted to take him on. I knew, though, that the shelter would put this tiny soul, blind, old, and with a tumor the size of a grapefruit descended from his testicle, to final sleep.

I said a prayer that none of the fleas would infest my house as we brought him down to the basement and started washing, and washing, and washing...

Through it all, Anthony stood quiet and still, not a growl or a twinge of struggle.

When we were done, this little light-brown Pomeranian lay very still, his tongue hanging sideways out of his mouth. I wasn't too hopeful.

My trusted vet was on vacation, so we brought him to another for an initial exam. We walked out with a $600 bill even before talk of the tumor. Were we crazy to invest so much in this little life?

X-rays found bones in his stomach. What a horrid life this little man must have led.

Yes, he was blind, partially deaf, had bad teeth—the usual array of old-age adversities. The vet couldn't say just how old he was for sure. The best estimation was at least 13-15 years of age.

A week passed, and he was alive, though not looking too well. My vet returned, and we brought Anthony to see him.

To my amazement, he said, "You know, I thought I was going to see him at death's door, but I see hope here. Do you want to take a chance and operate? Remove the testicles and see what happens?"

I looked down at this limp, little body, tongue hanging out of his mouth, and said, "Okay." This crazy lady said, "Yes," and Anthony lived three more years.

Never was there a growl, never one aggressive bone in his little body…including the ones in his stomach.

Anthony died peacefully at home with us, this little boy without sight, stranded on a busy highway….until my son gave him a chance at life.

- Seventeen -
Angel

Angel was just that, a little angel to me. He couldn't stay very long on this earth, but he will stay forever in my heart.

He was tied up in a blue garbage bag and left outside the shelter's door.

He was old; we could only guess just how old. The shelter ad said six or seven. Shelter ads are often like aging women who stretch the truth a bit. PJ, as he was dubbed by the shelter, was actually in his teen years. One look at his white, cataract-laden eyes, and I knew he was no adolescent.

He wobbled a bit, he was partially deaf, but he was my *trash treasure*...my pirate booty. He meant the world to me.

The vet said his heart was enlarged. How much time he had was questionable. Each day, when I walked up the path to my door, I listened for his little bark. It was my music of the day, for it told me he was still okay.

Angel endured much humiliation; he was just too cute for his own good. I dressed him up as a sunflower once. He endured it all for me.

Three months. That is all that Heaven would permit me. He went outside and just turned over sideways. His little lungs took one final breath in my arms.

A little ray of sun set in my heart that day.

- Eighteen -
Apache Tears

She wasn't intended to come home.

I went to the breeder's home to pick up my sable and white boy, the beautiful sheltie I had always wanted. I had picked him out online. We drove to get him that night.

He had no use for me; in fact, he let out a little puppy growl. The breeder said this meant nothing. "Puppies like you one minute and growl at you the next."

There were other boys; they were all waiting for their owners to come. In their midst stood a teeny girl. She was the runt of the litter.

"I don't know what will become of her. She doesn't like anyone."

The breeder called her possum girl. She was black and white with beautiful, blue eyes. A bi-blue in the sheltie world.

I picked her up. She lifted her paw for me. The deal was clinched.

I went for a big boy. I came home with a teeny girl. This was meant to be.

I named her Apache Tears for the beautiful obsidian stone. The legend of this stone teaches that whoever holds Apache Tears will shed no tears of her own. Legend claims Apache warriors flung themselves over the cliffs so as not to be captured by soldiers. The Apache mothers and wives wept over these cliff sides, and their tears solidified into obsidian.

Apache is a special girl. She is afraid of all things outside the house. She will only go outside long enough to relieve herself, and even then only a few feet from the safety of the steps. Then, she hurries back in. The garden gate might just as well be her cliff. She never walks on the leash. I have tried and tried to encourage her to explore the world, but her happiness lies within her safe walls of home.

Other families would not have tolerated such emotions and anxiety in a dog, but my possum girl knew with whom to hitch a ride home that night.

She remains my only girl in a pack full of boys, and she controls them all. No one gives any guff to my Apache girl. She is the boss within her walls.

She does not like problems or anxiety in her domain. If one of her brothers gets into trouble, the minute he is confronted with a reprimanding voice, Apache goes into her room and closes the door behind her. Every time she hears a dog's name being called for discipline, Apache follows this routine—walks to her room and shuts the door. It is her safe corner in a safe harbor away from the treacherous outside seas.

She saves all her fear for the world outside. Inside, she has dominion and control.

Apache Tears need not worry; I will keep her safe for all the days of her life. I promise she will shed no tears in fright.

- Nineteen -
Casper LambBear Highlander

Maybe it was all my childhood days sitting in front of the television screen watching *Lassie*. The wish for a collie had been imprinted on my heart.

I kept a picture of one in a heart frame in my kitchen for years. It was my "heart wish" to have a collie. I had a stuffed Lassie toy in my bedroom growing up. He was holding court until the real one came along. We had decided our home was not large enough for a collie's size, so I took home a sheltie instead. Apache is dearly loved, but my heart still longed for a collie.

One day, my "Butterfly Boy" came to me. He was a puppy born with a sable-colored butterfly across his back. Butterflies are the messengers of spirits. Casper's butterfly markings sent the message that he was meant for me.

He was a ball of fluff that I held in my lap for the entire ride home from New Hampshire to New Jersey. Looking at this massive fur ball, it is hard to imagine ever holding him in my lap.

Collies are the stoic, strong herders of the Scottish Highlands. I gave my boy a true Scottish name, a *play* on the actor who portrayed MacLeod in *The Highlander*. I tell that to my boy as he sticks his snout an inch out of my door and determines if the weather is suitable for his delicate paws. More times than not, the slightest dewdrop of moisture in the air is enough to send him running—running back in the house. The sheep in Scotland would all be free, especially in the rain.

My Casper would most likely be the one IN the well, not the one rescuing others. There are glimmers of his herding instinct, though, as he waits for all the other pack members in my yard to be rounded up and back inside.

His nickname is "Barky MacDougle." Everyone in the neighborhood knows the exact moment my boy steps outside. Collies like to bark, even to the extent of some owners de-barking them. I would not do that to Casper, though sometimes I wish he could keep our early morning walks a little more private.

But do I love him. He is my Collie, my defender, my companion, my gentle giant, my perfect LASSIE.

Casper suffers from a rare immunity disease. It cannot be cured, only managed. He has his good months and his not so good ones. But I will happily share each one with my "Butterfly Boy."

- Twenty -
Bram

Bram is a happy, little boy. We named him after Bram Stoker, the author of *Dracula*. On his car ride home, I noticed two little greyish markings, like fangs, beneath his mouth. From that moment on, he was Bram.

Bram was the equivalent of Dennis the Menace when he was a baby. We had a crate set up for him that was his time-out place. Bram had a lot of time-outs. We had a nickname for his crate; we called it the "mungee bin." Don't ask why—it just came to be. All we had to say was, "Bram! Mungee Bin!!!" and Bram would run in it by himself.

His penitent little face would creep close to the bars and mournfully plead for freedom, which was shortly granted. And then the mischief would begin again.

Bram has had a couple of seizures; thankfully, they have been few and far between.

If the phrase, *"He can get away with anything because he is cute,"* holds true, then Bram is the poster child.

Bram's nickname is Paul Revere; he is the house crier. At first peek of sunlight, Bram is barking, announcing the morning's arrival. Who needs an alarm clock? We have Bram.

Soon enough, he gets the whole house joining in. Some days, we beat the sun. The first creak of the bed, the first toe on the bedroom floor—these become the signals for Paul to announce the morning.

He takes his job seriously; he hasn't missed a day. And he works pretty cheaply. Just a little bowl of morning food is all that he requires to be happy.

If you have trouble hearing your morning alarm, get a little Pomeranian. You will never be late again.

- Twenty-One -
Gingersnap

Did you ever buy something you had no forethought in purchasing? It was the last thing you really needed, but you could not resist bringing it home anyway?

Such was the case with a little Cairn Terrier, like Toto from *The Wizard of Oz*. I had always loved little Toto. Perhaps my heart dreamed of having a little dog beside me on some future brick or concrete or dirt road in my future.

She was very unhappily circling her small cage in a strip mall pet shop in a nearby town. I peered in through the window of the shop and spotted her. The sign read, "Female Cairn Terrier," and a big sign placed in the front of the shop read, "Special—Half-Off Sale."

I believe in signs, in messages from the Universe that show you a tear in the Universe's curtain. You can venture through or seal it up tightly with patches.

I ventured through and bought her.

The pet shop owner was very terse and said, "She is final sale. You can't bring her back." All sales were final in my house; once a being came in, it never went back.

And so Gingersnap found my home. She was three-quarters into her first year, old for a pet shop puppy. I have since learned the horror stories of where these "unsellables" sometimes wind up. I am happy I saved her from such a fate.

I have no regrets, though she came with a train car filled with baggage. If there was something disgusting to eat or roll in, Ginger was there. Her girly habits left much to be desired. She snapped constantly—at the air and at us. Not biting, but snapping, like a snapping turtle. Hence her name, Gingersnap.

It took about a year for Ginger to finally stop snapping, but her circling and barking continued for life. It took about another year to finally get her to turn belly-up to be petted.

She truly was my *Girl from Oz*. Her papers said she came from a breeder in Kansas—most likely from a puppy mill.

She was the walking billboard for puppy mill misfits. Poorly bred, she developed Cushing's disease. She never truly learned bonding from the time of her birth. She was a friendly girl, but we could never let her off her leash. There was no division in friendliness toward us or friendliness to the people down the street. A little puppy learns this bonding from time spent at his or her siblings' and mother's side. Ginger obviously was torn away from this love before she learned what it truly was.

Ginger lived about 12 years with us and tried to be the best girl she could. She did have her moments...

When I called all the dogs inside from the yard, it was Ginger who paused, turned back to wait for me, and always walked in by my side. Perhaps she was thanking me for ending her unhappy wait for love in a wire cage so long before.

She will always be my Girl from Oz...............

- Twenty-Two -
Tad (The Heart Compares)

I recently adopted a little old man, roughly 90 years young in dog years. He was living at a small rescue in a rural area of Pennsylvania. So rural, in fact, that our GPS didn't guide us correctly there. We stopped our car, and I asked a Mennonite woman walking by if she knew of a place where dogs were rescued. She pointed down a road in the opposite direction, and there we found Nikki.

He was a little white Pomeranian who lived a life of hell-on-earth. One of those dogs you see carried out of hoaders' homes, encrusted with filth, excrement, and disease, beyond most human imagination. He had a deformed mouth, very crooked teeth, and an under bite reminiscent of a baby warthog. He wriggled like a worm in human arms, probably never held or loved before.

I renamed him Tad. Lincoln nicknamed his baby Tad because he squiggled like a little tadpole. Abe's little boy had such crooked teeth and a cleft palate that special foods had to be prepared for him. So the name fit, especially for this Gettysburg homeowner. Tad was so deaf, it really didn't matter what I renamed him. He responds to a very loud clapping of my hands most times—or the sight of the cookie bag.

He lived through starvation, pneumonia, and infestation of various kinds. He was not expected to pull through, but he did.

And six months later, I found him, or he found me...

What further makes this story heart-tugging is that this little Pomeranian is almost the mirror image of an "angel dog" that found me years before. Angel dogs are special companions; as Edith Wharton so eloquently wrote, "My little dog, a heartbeat at my feet." They are ones that make the largest holes in our hearts when they must bid farewell to the space beside our feet.

Naturally, when I saw Tad, I saw my angel dog Little Guy. It was bittersweet; I saw my Little Guy, but there was Tad. My heart wanted him to run to me and be the affectionate friend. Reality brought me the hurt little boy curled up in the corner.

Our hearts are great at comparing...comparing old boyfriends, comparing vacations, comparing the way a favorite old sweater fits "just right." It is hard not to compare, and old memory ghosts always seem to become more perfect as the years go by.

At first, part of my heart closed to him, even though much of my heart needed to engulf his stinky little body. I compared each move and each bite he took or did not take, the foods he liked, the corners in the home he favored—each moment in reality and memory.

Then, on a trip to a large pet store, a little, fuzzy lion hat waited on the Halloween display shelf. I bought it for another dog, thinking Tad was far too traumatized to enjoy a dress-up day. His Halloween horrors were "real."

But, some nudging from within made me attempt to put it on his head. And a magical thing occurred. As this tortured little dog looked up at me smiling, I knew the days of comparing had ended. For in that moment, I fell in love with Tad.

Tad has uniqueness about him. A solitary wanderer, he can be found just sitting in the yard for long periods of time, staring at the trees or sky.

A little dog who finds ecstasy in the trees, in the sky, in the breeze...

To watch this touching commune with nature reaches into a somewhat impenetrable place in most of our souls' secret corners. This being had never known the joys of outside and nature until a few months ago, having been cramped between cages of squalor and death.

He is estimated to be in his teen years, but Tad possesses wisdom beyond his years. I call him my "Little Thoreau," exploring the Walden Woods of my yard.

Others have noticed this about Tad. One can't help but be captivated by this "nature spirit." I have another dog that is very attuned to the Spirit World. My Tad is attuned to the world of Fairies and Dryads and Sprites. He is happiest among the garden pixies...in his own little corner of the "woods."

The air of quiet beauty surrounds him as he sits there, contemplating the mysteries of a mysterious life, fraught with unimaginable horrors.

I hope Tad is at peace amidst the small patch of woods outside my home. It is not the number of trees, but the beauty you find in each one.

"You only need sit still long enough in some attractive spot in the woods that all its inhabitants may exhibit themselves to you by turns." - Henry David Thoreau, *Walden*

- Twenty-Three -
Ozzy (Nine Days of Love)

I read about it all the time—two friends surrendered to the shelter, one adopted, one left behind.

My heart cries for the one *left behind*, watching his bonded friend go off with a strange family, wondering why they left him or her behind on the cold, damp shelter floor.

Animals bond. I have seen this especially with my birds. When one falls ill, the bonded mate spreads his wings around the other and encloses the bird in what can only be described as love. I have seen newly mateless birds pace back and forth along the perch, pining for a lost friend.

Dogs and cats feel this loss, too. Who hasn't seen the one left behind search through the house, longing to find a friend who made the journey first? Sometimes, the ones left behind leave soon after. I find it hard to dispute that heartache and grief played a part in their passing.

I once read the most touching story of a pair of dogs at a shelter, deeply attached friends. Their story is one of nothing less than love.

One night, the shelter attendant left the gate unlocked to this pair's enclosure. This was one of those outside shelters, where forlorn animals face the elements of nature. One dog was considerably larger than the other. The little dog managed to squeeze through a hole in the outer fence that led the way to freedom and escape from certain death. The bigger dog could not fit. Evidently, there was some type of security camera that captured what ensued.

The smaller dog waited and waited, hoping some miracle might free his friend. Dawn came, and the little dog squeezed back inside the fence to be with his friend. The saddest part of the story is that the two dogs were soon euthanized, but shelter workers let them cross together.

I cannot separate bonds. I have adopted friends. To me, there is no other choice; in my mind and heart, the eyes of the one left behind would haunt me.

The fright of being dumped is insurmountable enough; without the comfort of a bonded sibling, it would be impossible to bear.

I know that rescues and shelters have to sometimes think in terms of saving one life rather than none at all. Sadly, though, this is sometimes at the expense of love and friendship. My heart always cries when I see two together that may soon be one.

The eyes of frightened friends behind the bars of a cage are the saddest eyes of all. Their eyes cry to my heart. I wish more people would see into those eyes and realize how much love they truly feel.

As I mentioned before, Tad came from a hoarder's house. Upon her death, Tad was found amongst the filth and stench, so covered in flea infestation that he had lost much of his fur and was near death with pneumonia.

When I called the shelter, they said Tad had come in with a friend, also furless and much older (which is tough because Tad is thirteen). Ozzy was blind, deaf, and also recovering from near fatal pneumonia. He had lost all of his fur, but it had grown back beautifully during his convalescence.

The shelter staff jokingly asked if I would consider taking both of them. They didn't know me.

I took them both. Tad and his brother Ozzy came home with me.

Ozzy was so old and frail, even the shelter volunteer didn't think he had much time. More around seventeen or eighteen, his battle with pneumonia had siphoned most of the strength from his little body.

Safely home, he enjoyed two great days of eating and staking out a quiet place to nap ninety-nine percent of the day. I forgot what homemade food I gave him that first meal, but he ate with such gusto. I don't think he had ever tasted more than a few kernels of dry kibble.

But on day three, Ozzy faltered. I could see him fading.

I like to think he was peaceful at last and could let go. I hope he thought he had already found a warm little spot on the Bridge. His eyes and ears had long darkened, so his senses could only *feel* love and warmth and a belly satisfied as he lay sleeping.

I wish Ozzy could have stayed. I told him he had a home for life, for however long he chose to remain.

He stayed nine days. Nine days of love, and safety, and a quiet place to rest his head, knowing what it felt like to be cared about before he left this earth.

Do I regret taking on a heartache I knew would soon come? No. Ozzy was the sweetest, gentlest soul. He was meant to make my home his stop on the way to Rainbow Bridge.

One day, Tad and I will find him waiting there. Sometimes, I think Tad is still communicating with his brother as he sits quietly among the trees in my yard.

Nine days can equal a lifetime of love—and a lifetime of remembrance in this owner's heart.

- Twenty-Four -
Do Animals Feel Grief?

I've often wondered if Tad felt grief over his brother Ozzy's death.

I once had an interesting conversation with an animal expert on the subject of animal grief. His viewpoint, though very erudite, differed from mine.

To him, prey animals did not have time for grief; therefore, they did not display it.

From my time as a zoo docent, I learned the differences among the prey animals, i.e. the deer, the African gazelles, the grazers who had to diligently keep eyes glues on the horizon for predators intent on eating them.

That is why, in his words, a deer can watch a fawn hit by a car and run off, no time for grief. It simply does not exist in the *prey world*.

He explained that the larger animals, the ones not concerned with being someone's next meal, could feel grief. The elephants, for instance, have the time to mourn over the bodies and bones of family members since they need not be worried about who is eyeing them as a next meal.

I disagree. I believe they all know grief, but some have the luxury of allowing time to express it in a world of danger and death.

I never forgot the story I once read of a mother doe that watched her fawn hit by a car and ran frantically back and forth, back and forth, along the highway. Finally, she ran directly into traffic and ended her life, as well.

If not a mother's grief, what is the explanation for this?

I truly believe, from my experience as an Animal Communicator, that they do feel grief. Grief over the death of offspring and, as in the human world, grief over the death of owners and siblings that share their household as beloved pets.

Did you know that distress over the illness of an owner can many times exhibit similar illness in a pet? I have come across this in my work as a Reiki Master, sometimes treating pets for the same afflictions as their loved ones.

Why is this? Is the pet trying to take over the illness, feeling such grief over his or her owner's pain and worry?

Many times, owners would contact me about a pet that wouldn't eat, lost its zest for life, and became despondent. Often, these owners had just lost another pet in the home. Pets miss their companions; they grieve over the loss of a friend just as we do. Read stories of Greyfriars Bobby or

Hatchi and learn about the loyalty and grief of a companion's heart.

In my heart, I do believe that, in a quiet spot, momentarily safe from a predator's eye and mouth, all animals, even the ones preyed upon, shed sorrows of grief. We see our pets shed sorrow, but far away from watchful eyes, all beings shed tears of the heart.

- Twenty-Five -
Buddy

Day after day, I see whiskers, muzzles, and snouts of loneliness and fear posted across the social networking pages of the Internet.

Some greying, some still puppy or kitten-sized—all with ticking countdowns toward death. Postings warn of 24 hours left. To be killed. Immediate rescue needed. So many *earth angels* desperately trying to save them. But there are so many to be saved. Too many, sadly, will be escorted to a final room, a one-way journey.

Each time I look upon their longing eyes and sorrowful faces, I see my Buddy.

He was transported, thankfully, by a kind *earth angel* from a kill shelter in Virginia, shortly before his time had *run out.*

I call Bud my "Clara Barton," for he is the nursemaid to any who need comfort. Buddy's siblings never have a dirty face or ear when he is around.

If one is feeling under the weather, *Clara* is right there to the rescue. There is not a thread of meanness woven into Bud's body. He will share—no, *relinquish*—whatever he has without the tiniest of growls or confrontation.

Bud is so gentle that he is abused by some, namely Bailey. You'll read about him soon enough. Bailey will take advantage of Bud's sweetness and usurp his food bowl if my watchful eyes are diverted elsewhere.

If there is an incident to be framed for, Bud is the victim, the fall guy. He is left standing alongside the evidence of someone else's mischief. Yes, Bud is always framed for the crime. If anyone in the home is disciplined, Buddy shares the grief. He is my empath in the house and will carry his burden of sulkiness for any other's crime.

It took my Bud about six months to bark. He never uttered a sound when we brought him home. When he finally felt *at home,* a deep resounding woof emerged to announce his arrival, and he has become the sentry of our house. It was one of the nicest sounds to hear.

Buddy loves squirrels. Poor squirrels—if he ever caught one, the little critter would probably face death by face and ear licking.

Yes, when I look upon all those homeless, unloved faces without an angel waiting to take them for a drive toward survival, my heart aches. It might have been my sweet Bud walking instead toward the cold, back room of the shelter toward death.

- Twenty-Six -
Smokey

Smokey, a.k.a. the "Smokeman."

Newest member of the pack, Smokey came to live with us upon the death of my father-in-law. My father-in-law's biggest worry was what would happen to Smokey when he passed away from a terminal cancer. When he entered hospice, we took Smokey and promised we would take care of him as our own.

Smokey is the *James Dean* of Shiba Inus, a "Rebel without a Cause." But Smokey's rebellious nature had cause; he was suffering grief, too. He was extremely bonded with his dad. I know the separation from home and loved one has been as distressing for him as the upheaval his introduction into our family pack has been for us.

Don't be fooled by his James Dean good looks, although they will surely charm you.

Smokey has always been king of his domain, with a treasure cache of only his toys, only his bones, only his food. He came with dietary requirements fit for a king. Lettuce, peas, carrots, cottage cheese, applesauce, and a small helping of special dog food adorn his dinner bowl. Yes, to say Smokey had been spoiled would be an understatement.

Saying Smokey is a problem child would also be an understatement. He was an obedience school flunkie, suspended because the trainers deemed him *untrainable.*

That's not correct; he has us pretty well trained.

He is a bundle of muscle. Shibas are the snow dogs of Japan. Outdoor behavior leaves much to be desired in Smokey; he looks upon each passing car as a victim waiting to be attacked. Walking Smokey on a leash is not recommended, unless you wish to be dragged as if you were the snow sled.

He once disappeared at one corner of my father-in-law's snow-laden yard, tunneled across, and reappeared at the opposite end, head popping out through the snow.

His favorite toys? Bricks. He carried my father-in-law's bricks around the yard, talking to them in his unique Shiba way, artistically arranging his masterpiece of the day.

Shibas talk. Go to YouTube and type in "Shiba." They are usually the ones saying, "I wuv you," in a Shiba dialect only owners swear they understand.

And they scream. Their vocal diversity takes some getting used to. Merely barking is not enough for a Shiba. Just the simple act of brushing can cause vocal screams to erupt, comparable to those of one being tortured on the rack.

He likes close-up communication. Some evenings, my husband would sleep over at his dad's and awaken to find a Shiba pair of eyes inches away from his head, just staring at him.

With his soft, fuzzy face only inches from your head, he can be endearing as he laments, "Hey lady, I didn't ask to come live with you either."

Yes, this Shiba can be charming, but beware. Underneath that handsome tuft of fur and smiling set of teeth lurks a rebel.

Who knows? If I ever need to tunnel out of my yard during a snowstorm, Smokey may come in handy.

- Twenty-Seven -
Bailey Gargoyle, My Alien Pom

Bailey needs a whole series of volumes to explain, but I will give a brief overview of adventures with this Pomeranian/alien mix.

Bailey came to me from a close friend whose daughter was challenged with life circumstances that made owning a dog no longer conceivable.

Bailey is a challenge. He fits in two environments—my home and some alien settlement on Mars. I think that is where he came from, though his papers claim somewhere in the Midwest.

My Bailey. Midwest, yes. Midwest of Saturn.

Bailey sees spirits. My friend knew this; she kept quiet and waited for me to say something. When I did, she exclaimed that he was meant to come to me.

Bailey's domain is the second floor of my home. One week, Bailey refused to go up the stairs. At night-time, my husband had to carry him reluctantly to our bedroom to sleep. I knew he sensed something was awry; there was a presence he did not feel comfortable near. When the energy cleared, he was back running up the stairs to bed.

Sometimes, he can be seen staring over our shoulders, perhaps looking at unseen friends from his alien birthplace.

Bailey lives by the creed, *"If it drops, I will eat it."* Once, I dropped my used tea bag on the kitchen floor. Bailey, usually my shadow in the kitchen, dive- bombed for it and, without thought, proceeded to chew. The look on his face would have captured the Funniest Home Video prize. That will always be my picture that *got away.* His expression of, "What the **** is this!!!!!!" was priceless!

I gave him a middle name; I call him Bailey Gargoyle. To me, his face looks like those guardians of Notre Dame.

I should write his name BAILEY. Remember those mothers from the neighborhoods of youth who could be heard screaming the names of delinquent children late in coming home? That's me, screaming Bailey's name to come in from the yard. Just like on *Cheers*, everybody knows his name.

- Twenty-Eight -
Close Encounters of the Fourth Kind
(Life with Bailey)

The mischief and mayhem Bailey causes could fill the NASA Blue Book of Aliens.

I have come to the understanding that there is, indeed, some type of alien hybrid hidden in his genetic code.

Bailey does not speak Canine, English, or any other language. Communicating with him is a one-way street, and that is a dead end. Usually my communication reveals itself in the high-toned yell, "BAILEY," that emanates from the house countless times during the day.

Morning breakfasts bring the same scenario to my house—everyone eating peacefully until Bailey dive-bombs (like an alien saucer) into everyone's bowl. With one incredulous leap, he can stuff his alien Pom cheeks with a whole bowl of food. I don't know how he does it.

Could it be a race of Pom-sized alien chipmunks has landed somewhere and disguised themselves as Poms? Only the giant chipmunks and one alien Pom know for sure, and they are not communicating.

One particular morning will live in infamy in my brain.

It was very early morning; Paul Revere had sounded his alarm, and my husband had taken everyone out.

I was in bed, still groggy. It was still not quite light outside. Bailey came running upstairs and paused at the side of my bed. I had my arm hung over the side, and my hand just grazed the feel of what I first perceived as a twig in Bailey's mouth.

But this didn't feel right; it felt too squishy to be a twig.

A second of dread coursed through my mind as I called to my husband to see what Bailey had.

Bailey had a mole in his mouth. I had felt those mushy feelers that extend from their snouts with my hands. He dropped its poor lifeless body on my bedroom floor. It was my worst nightmare. I ran to the bathroom screaming and putting my arms into the sink filled with sudsy water. I know, not great behavior for an Animal Communicator, but I had no wish to have an early morning connection with a dead mole in my dark bedroom.

Alas, that mole was not to be the last. We found Bailey with another victim in our dining room a few months later. The moles in our garden must have sent out their own communication memo.

Bailey never found another one after that. They learned that my yard, with an alien Pom, was not a safe place to tunnel.

Bailey took up the reins from my girl Ginger quite proficiently. If there is something disgusting to eat, to roll around in, or to regurgitate on my floor or sofa, he will do it.

I don't think there is another human family willing to put up with this extraterrestrial problem. He is ours—at least until his mother spaceship comes to claim him again.

- Twenty-Nine -
Mr. Jingles

You don't have to bark to be welcomed into my house of misfits. Squeaks, squawks, chirps, and rabbit thumps are allowed, too.

Choosing a name for a pet is an important decision. Sometimes, the name you pick winds up being the perfect one. So is the case of my Mr. Jingles.

My friend had purchased two dwarf hamsters, and lo and behold, the female was pregnant. I adopted one of the little baby boys and named him Mr. Jingles after the mouse in *The Green Mile*.

I never would have imagined how close a bond a little *mouse* and I could create. Each morning, at the sound of his name, his tiny head emerged from his woven nest to greet the day and his breakfast blueberry. My kids teased that no one ate until Mr. Jingles got his carrots and blueberry. He had a special spaceship cage with levels and slides and, of course, his little wheel. He had his own special race car wheel; as he spun around, the car moved across the floor. Yes, he was loved and happily spoiled as much as a little hamster could possibly be.

One blueberry each day—that was Mr. Jingles' favorite treat. He was a tiny little fur ball who brought a burst of sunshine into my life each morning. But not for long.

In a few months, he became quite ill. We took him to the vet and got medication to treat what perhaps was one of the viruses that can so easily take hold of such tiny bodies. The vet said he either loved or hated seeing these little guys as patients. He could tell which ones were properly cared for and socialized; Mr. Jingles was a delight to him. He let the vet hold him and examine him with no trouble. No biting, as many little ones who aren't held daily will show to the hands that attempt to hold them.

Daily doses of medication given by eyedropper seemed to make him well again; my Mr. Jingles got a second chance at life, just like the little mouse revived in the movie. But the virus came back (or never really left). The second round of medication did not have the same effect.

He grew weaker and weaker. He didn't greet me with his sunny smile or wait for his morning blueberry or his saucer of grated vegetables anymore. Then, his tiny body lapsed into a coma. Alive, but just existing, he lay very still for a couple of days. I still gave him medication by eyedropper, but my boy was fading.

As I held him the last time, he suddenly opened his eyes. He looked directly into mine. I know he was saying he loved me and goodbye. The next instant, he closed them and took one last breath. Then, he was gone.

That little hamster broke my heart as deeply as any other pet I had ever loved. Others would jest at just how much love a little hamster as tiny as this could give to an owner. I know otherwise; I saw the look in his eyes as he lay dying. He woke to say goodbye to me.

This little being, only ounces in size, succeeded in carrying off my heart with him on his journey to the Bridge.

- Thirty -
Val

It took me quite a while to want another little dwarf hamster. Then Valentine's Day arrived, and my daughter got me Val, named for the day and for Val Kilmer.

I went into this new relationship doubtful that my heart could be won over again. But, as fate would have it, Val became as entrenched in my heart as deeply as Mr. Jingles. He let me carry him around and filled the tiny hole of grief left by his former cage resident.

But, even under the best of circumstances, these little beings don't live long. Months go by quickly, and their time with us ends much too soon.

I knew at the end Val was leaving. I took him outside, sat him in the sunlight, and let him enjoy its warmth on his body. I think all beings should enjoy the sun and the grass at least once before they leave this earth.

I once read a story of a woman who raised a tiny mouse. As he lay dying, she placed his tiny body on a flower in the grass so he might feel the wonder of the world.

I never forgot this. I have let my tiny friends lie in the grass and feel the sun before their time with me ended, as well.

Once, I had a beloved little dwarf bunny named Daffodil. The vet said nothing could be done for him, and we left the office to let him pass at home. I talked with him on the way home, telling him to wait until we got there.

When we got home, I laid his tiny body in the grass. He died there. I planted a row of daffodils on the spot where his soul left; each spring, I see them and remember him.

Val spent his last afternoon in the sun, as well. He died peacefully in his cage later that day.

Years have passed. I have never gotten another dwarf hamster. I am not afraid I will not find another Mr. Jingles or Val. Perhaps I am afraid I will. My heart cannot bear to lose another.

- Thirty-One -
Silver Belle, Buttons, Bunny, and Chip

The earth's creatures share much with us humans. They share kindness and empathy, and they share cruelness and sorrow.

Birds are very intelligent creatures. It is no wonder that they share a dark side like their human counterparts.

I once shared my home with a little cockatiel named Silver Belle. I used to sing the Christmas tune of the same name to her all year round. I miss her, especially when Christmas comes and this song plays...

Silver Belle laid many beautifully-sculpted white eggs a few years after I brought her home. They weren't fertile, of course; she never seemed to know what to do with them.

I decided to get her a mate for companionship.

For more than a year, Buttons and Belle seemed to tolerate each other. I often saw Buttons vying for her affection—a lost cause, I'm afraid. Belle wanted not much to do with him. He would perch close to her, speak his cockatiel endearments to her, and she would quickly slide over to the nearest corner of the cage.

Instead of *my intention* (of bringing her the closeness of a mate), I just provided a roommate for her, and she, instead, grew closer to me.

The two of them lived peacefully together like two buddies—nothing more. Silver Belle looked to me to hold her and love her and keep her safe. This makes the mystery even sadder, for I could not keep my beloved girl safe.

One morning, I heard the most horrifying scream from the cage. I was on the other side of the house. By the time I ran there, my Silver Belle was lying on the cage floor, her eyes looking up at me in sadness.

My beautiful Silver Belle...I watched her die.

For some reason, Buttons had attacked her. For what, I do not know. Maybe just because she didn't love him.

I still have Buttons. We have an understanding and forgiveness. Although he caused me great heartache, I promised to care for him and keep him safe, as well, and I have kept my promise. He lives by himself in his cage; I would never chance such incident again, and he seems happy by himself, holding dominion over his space.

Birds are a lot like people. Love can cause tremendous acts of kindness; unrequited love can cause tremendous acts of rage.

I miss Silver Belle, the pretty girl I sang to, especially when the holidays come and that Christmas standard is played.

Buttons talks. Sometimes, I walk into the room and hear a little voice tell me, "I'm a good boy."

Perhaps it's the voice of a little bird's sorrow, asking forgiveness from my heart.

After Belle died, I was heart-broken. My dad asked my daughter to find me another cockatiel, and she brought home Chip. As I sat with this little bird on my shoulder, I sought the perfect name for him. Then it occurred to me. I was holding a *chip on my shoulder.* And so his name became Chip.

As there are no coincidences, the name Chip was even more perfect than I first thought. The little broken dish in *Beauty and the Beast* is named Chip; so his name gave even more meaning to my little Belle. As Chip grew, his personality changed (as many times is the case in birds). They are so intelligent; each has a personality all its own. Some are friendly, some can be ornery and grumpy, and some can be downright nasty. Chip, as his name implies, has a continual "chip on his shoulder" and faces most days with grumpiness.

Bunny hitchhiked to our humble abode with my daughter on one of her visits home from college.

Walking back from class one day toward the end of the semester, my daughter heard a recognizable chirp that reminded her of home. There, walking on the path that led to her dormitory, was a cockatiel.

The other students didn't know what kind of bird he was. Not my daughter—she'd been raised with enough of a flock to know he was a cockatiel. Maybe someone tossed him out of a window to fly away once the semester was over.

He is my Johnny Cash of cockatiels; instead of Sue, this boy has Bunny as his name. Perhaps that is why he shares Chip's grumpiness. He couldn't tell me his name, but he sure talked a blue streak when we brought him home. "Pretty, pretty, pretty boy" could be heard broadcasted around the house, as well as, "I'm a good bird." Bunny could imitate the ring of my phone so precisely that I often came running through the house to answer. When I coughed, Bunny coughed.

Bunny shares his room now with Chip and Buttons, each in his own cage. They are like little kids. When the phone rings, they like to start screaming, the same way kids act up when moms are on the phone. Just try to watch a favorite movie; they seem to know and start their antics just as the first scene unfolds.

Birds are a big commitment; they live for decades. You never know the personality you will end up with. Birds go through the *terrible twos* toddler stage. Sometimes they grow out of it; sometimes they stay grumpy. Realize that you may be sharing your home with a grumpy old man for many, many years before you bring a bird in to share your life.

- Thirty-Two -
A Christmas Eve Birth

I love doves. I have been privileged to share my home with many. Their mournful calls offer a comfort and peace to my mornings and nights.

A bonded pair of white doves that I rescued holds a special place in my heart. They were tossed away, without a given reason, and a friend who took them in gave them to me. It took me a while to learn the reason why, but soon, the answer was revealed.

Most raise doves for breeding purposes. Doves for weddings, doves for magic shows. Therefore, an infertile pair of doves is not a financial asset. My pair of doves seemed to be infertile. Perhaps they were siblings. The female laid egg after egg, all infertile. I usually left the pair to tend to these yolk-filled shells. They were excellent parents, keeping their treasures safe and warm.

Then, on a magical Christmas Eve several years ago, I woke to a cracked shell in the bottom of the cage. The rim of blood foretold the father dove's secret.

Beneath him slept a teeny baby. My Christmas Eve baby.

Shortly thereafter, I knew something was not right. This little baby was deformed.

I cared for him as best as I could, trying to get him to eat, trying to keep him clean. The doves were excellent parents, too. They tended to him for several weeks and then finally let him be.

Birds and animals in the wild have a sixth sense about these things; they know who can and who cannot survive.

After a few weeks, this little bald peanut had blossomed into a full white-feathered, beautiful dove, but deformity made it impossible for his parents to care for him any longer. My human efforts failed; my baby dove went back to heaven, dying with wings outstretched in a final attempt to learn how it felt to fly. I believe my beautiful little dove did fly above the clouds that day.

They have had one more baby since then with the same deformity. Although my heart sank, I helped them tend to the inevitable. Now my babies have each other amidst the clouds of heaven. Two beautiful white doves to fly in the celestial sky.

Fortunately, this story has a happy ending. These wonderful parents went on to help raise a wild dove. They enabled him to live and learn to fly. They accepted another bird's thrown away baby and gave the gift of life to one other than their own.

So my beautiful doves rescue, as well. The life you rescue may one day rescue you or another.

There is treasure found in things thrown away—sometimes monetary, sometimes more priceless.

- Thirty-Three -
Canaries

Canaries are encoded in my heart; I think it is genetics. I once found a story of an ancestor who held a funeral procession through town for his beloved canary.

I love their song. Most don't know that it isn't a song of happiness; rather, it's the longing for a mate.

I have kept canaries in solitary cages, and I have kept them in pairs. Once, a little female canary built the most extraordinary nest of computer paper she had moistened with water. It was a masterpiece. When she passed away, I buried her sitting within it.

I have had so many canary friends over the years. Their fragility often brings heartache. I have lost many suddenly and others after long, weakening illnesses.

Sunflower was a special little boy. He enjoyed Irish folksongs and reels. Each day, I would play one particular song on my CD player, and he would accompany the entire song with his beautiful melodies.

Wolfie was another favorite. I named him Wolfman or "Wolfie" because he had a circle of feathers on top of his head. I had another boy like him called Moe, after Moe of the Three Stooges (same hairstyle). Wolfie was the only canary who climbed upon my hand and ate his favorite treat—shredded carrots. Losing him was especially heart-breaking.

A canary will bring such happiness to your heart but will also bring such sadness when its voice becomes silent. I have discovered one amazing occurrence. Before they die, canaries will sing the most beautifully. It is as if they are giving one last song to the world. I have heard it many times.

Such is often the case in the animal world. Before death, an animal will suddenly show a renewed spark for life. Many times, pet owners will call and tell me of this when animals I have treated with Reiki are very ill and near the end of life. I remain silent; I do not tell them what I know. Why destroy the last moments of happiness these beloved animals share with those they love? It is their final gift to us.

All of them, each tiny feathered being, will remain in my heart forever. Their songs are encoded in my heart.

- Thirty-Four -
Midnight

Having my Reiki practice brought a few adoptees to my door. People would bring me wild birds they found, not having the time or knowledge of how to care for them. Sometimes, I got bunnies.

One such adoptee was a black, Angora dwarf bunny. I named him Midnight.

The woman who brought him to my office said she *found* him on a neighbor's lawn. She tried to keep him, but she changed her mind.

I didn't ask many questions, though I wondered why she would go out and buy such an expensive cage and all accessories for this bunny and quickly change her mind. A lot of times, people who buy rabbits will change their minds. Rabbits are a lot of work. They need attention and care to keep their messy cages clean and their fur, especially of an Angora, in good condition.

Midnight wasn't in good condition. But, he was the gentlest bunny I ever owned. He lived several years with me and never had to fear fending for himself out in the wild again.

Rabbits have very distinct personalities, some more friendly than others. Rabbits can even growl. Most people do not know this. I have a tiny girl bunny who likes to growl in annoyance each time I reach my hand in to clean her cage. She is *all growl and no bite*; she just doesn't like to be held.

Midnight never once uttered a growl, never showed any sign of nastiness or annoyance. He was just the sweetest bunny one could ever hope to know.

How his previous owner had found him didn't matter; all that mattered was he found me and his home.

- Thirty-Five -
Friend

Perhaps my family's most dramatic rescue story is that of Friend.

Friend is my daughter's bunny. He has a permanent head tilt. We are experienced with this condition in rabbits, as another of our bunnies had this affliction. But Friend happened by his in a unique way.

Friend was one of the pet bunnies found wandering outside. He was probably dropped off by owners who no longer saw the cuteness, only the care and expense involved in caring for a bunny.

A woman had seen Friend wandering through her yard for a couple of days. Then, horrified, she watched a hawk swoop down and attempt to carry him off. The hawk dropped Friend, badly injuring him and leaving him with a head tilt.

The distraught woman called a rescue, and they took Friend to the vet's. Friend was covered in bulges holding larvae that had burrowed under his skin and hatched. These living bulges had to be surgically removed.

No one even expected him to live after the stress of being carried by a hawk. But he lived, and he has been flourishing for over a year now.

The beginning wasn't easy; Friend wasn't neutered. The vet felt it too risky to attempt this added operation. So, Friend would spray, marking his cage and beyond with urine. Then, he started biting.

The only remedy was neutering; the vet said this was the only answer. Thankfully, it was. Friend became a different boy after the surgery.

Since he had been through so much, I am glad he found his way to my daughter, who would give him every last chance for happiness as her *friend.*

- Thirty-Six -
Chickens Get Rescued, Too

"Did you lose a chicken?"

My son-in-law's dad thought he had rescued a wild turkey from the clutches of feral cats. Now, he doesn't live in a rural area, though wild turkeys are sometimes seen where the boundaries of country and city mesh. We looked up Internet pictures and decided this was indeed a young gobbler.

Not knowing what else to do, he fed this young survivor bread, and it thrived for a few days. But, the little bird's health and spark of life started to decline soon after.

The young turkey was loaded up in the car and driven to a wild bird sanctuary where the volunteers told him, "This does not qualify as a wild bird rescue. It is a chicken." Rescue volunteers sent the unlikely pair home again together, with a bag of chicken feed, after chastising him for giving bread as nourishment. One would hope they would have taken this needy mouth and fed it and nourished it right then and there; but alas, this was not the sanctuary "procedure."

So the man and the newly-dubbed chicken drove home together again.

Now, as this houseguest grew, it "came more to light" that cluck was indeed more appropriate. This little feathered friend was indeed more likely to wind up in Mr. Perdue's farm than Tom Turkey's. Its little "chickenhood" was emerging more and more each day.

So the chicken and my son-in-law's dad lived together still, the little survivor thriving on the feed. My son-in-law's dad still faced the quandary of what to do with a chicken in a suburban backyard once winter came.

Desperate for a solution, my son's dad (I will shorten the in-law as this basically is just a title for one who has become another son) came up with a brilliant idea. He would start walking the neighborhood, ringing doorbells and asking, "Did you lose a chicken?"

Now, if this wasn't my animal rescuing family, this might sound bizarre. To a bunch of neighbors, this might sound insane. It is lucky this man wasn't cuffed and hauled off in a squad car.

But wait, fairy tale endings do come to chickens, for the "Prince" found the rightful owner of her/his chicken foot. He rang a doorbell and asked, "Did you lose a chicken?" And the owner said, "YES!"

Waiting in the the backyard was a pen of chickens who I am sure were just as surprised to see this little stray come home as the person who answered the door.

I, myself, would think my chances of seeing a huge check with a bunch of balloons attached at my door is more plausible than someone saying, "Did you lose a chicken?"

The truth is often stranger than fiction...

Part Three

Spiritual Snippets

- Thirty-Seven -
Charm

When my niece was 29 years young, we lost her to cancer. It was a horrible cancer; it caused suffering and disfigurement before stealing her life from her.

My niece loved Halloween. Every year, the cousins would get together to celebrate her favorite holiday.

And, she loved cats.

I spoke of my brother's connection with cats earlier. This was his child.

Theresa died two weeks before Halloween. Everyone was dreading this holiday that year. Even at her funeral, the bouquets were adorned with Halloween decorations, as tribute to her fondness for this time of year.

Halloween Eve, Mischief Day, I saw him in my yard under a lilac bush.

I had never seen such a beautiful cat; he was not of this world. His long, silky, black coat was matched by the most supernatural eyes I had ever looked into.

He did not run, but he did not like me getting too close either. I left him under the bush, and went inside. I came back out again, and he was still there, resting, so I let him be.

This was a side area of my yard where my pack of dogs had no access, so he was peaceful.

That evening, I took the dogs out in the yard and looked for him. He was not under the bush. But something made me look and find him elsewhere.

The rear of my home has a lattice enclosed crawlspace where we store wood, wire Christmas reindeer, and the likes here. I saw him in the crawlspace, peering at me through the lattice. He seemed unscathed by the running and barking of my dogs close to his new domain.

At first, I thought maybe he was ill or hurt and needed sanctuary. I put out some tuna—all that I had in the house that might tempt him—and a water dish. I slid them under the lattice entryway.

The next morning, he was there. And he stayed there for one entire week. I even went grocery shopping for cat food. I would wake up bright and early to feed him, and he would be there waiting. At night, I left his dinner.

I never would have imagined a cat would feel safe surrounded by dogs of all sizes and shapes, running and barking in the yard. But it was as if they could not see him. I sometimes wonder if they could. The picture I have is the closest he would let me capture, his head peering intently at me through the edge of the latticework. You cannot see his body, but you can see his unearthly eyes.

I called him Charm because he was my magical totem. I believe Theresa brought him to ease the pain of Halloween that year.

I never saw him before that week; I have never once seen him after. He totally vanished into thin air, returning for whence he came.

I genuinely believe he was not of this earth. He had to leave when his mission and message were accomplished. His message was to let me know that my niece lived on, somewhere, in another place, with a magical cat by her side.

- Thirty-Eight -
Winged Messengers

Butterflies are revered by many cultures as the winged messengers of the Spirit World. I truly believe they are.

When the cobwebs of my mind need dusting, I go walking. There is a walking track near my home. Here, the winds clear away those cobwebs and send the dust particles back into the Universe and out of my mind.

On this particular day, some cobwebs needed dusting.

Six years to this day, my 29-year-old niece, Theresa, passed away from cancer of the mouth, an agonizing, horrendous way to cross.

First, they removed part of her tongue.

The next operation removed a good number of her teeth.

A pretty young girl…I cannot imagine the suffering she endured. She endured much. She fought. She had a little boy in kindergarten; he was her reason to battle.

Shortly before she died, she handed her mother a piece of paper. She couldn't talk anymore.

The note asked, "Am I going to die?"

I don't know what her mother responded. There are some questions one need not ask.

On the day of her death, I started walking the track. It cleared my mind, and there were countless cobwebs to clear. Cobwebs of grief, of anger, of disbelief, all intertwining and tangling my thoughts.

I didn't know what else to do but walk, and I walked each morning.

At her wake, I sat with her little boy in a side room at the funeral parlor. He colored a Winnie the Pooh page out of his coloring book of a yellow butterfly. I wish I had torn that page out and kept it, but I didn't want to disturb his book. I have not seen him in many years; her husband left with him soon after her death.

The day of her burial, we walked over to my mother's grave, a grave decorated by a granddaughter and her little boy to the great grandma he never knew. Ceramic frogs basked in the sunlight, and pinwheels fluttered in the breeze.

I cried at how such a thing could happen, and a monarch butterfly flew across the grave. The day we buried my mother, a monarch flew across her grave. Now, he came back to tell me my niece and mother were together.

I knew this was my mother; butterflies are the messengers of the spirits.

I went home and went to the track.

While I was walking, a little yellow butterfly flew up in front of me and seemed to be my companion. I smiled and jokingly asked, "Hey, Theresa, I know that's you. Where's my mom?"

Immediately, a large monarch butterfly joined the yellow one, and the two seemed to dance in the air around me.

I heard fellow walkers muttering on the track to look at that..."*those butterflies are dancing.*"

I knew what *that* was.

Days later, I walked the track again to clear more lingering cobwebs. So immersed in thought, I stared down at the pavement until I looked up and saw, fluttering beside me, a pretty, little yellow butterfly.

"I guess my mom was busy off on adventures with my dad. They have a lot of catching up to do."

I called out, "Hi Theres" and smiled. "I will never forget your boy. Someday, he might come looking for us, and I will tell him this story, probably as we go for a little walk."

Then, years of cobwebs, separation, and grief will all be blown to the Universe, perhaps carried off by butterfly wings.

- Thirty-Nine -
The Oldest Pet Cemetery

Nearly 125 years ago, a veterinarian allowed a beloved dog to be buried in his apple orchard. Thus began the oldest and most honored pet cemetery, located in Upstate New York— Hartsdale Pet Cemetery, a place of tranquility and remembrance.

My visit to Hartsdale happened on a cold and drizzly day. I love drizzly days in cemeteries. The photos capture the grey atmosphere, justified by the greyness of the stones and the wistfulness of lives that now lay at rest.

I have some beautiful photos of Hartsdale, but I will never show them publicly. That is a rule at Hartsdale, to uphold the privacy of those who have entrusted their beloved companions to rest upon this orchard. One must sign a promise to never show them, and that is a promise I keep.

The stones range from modest to sublime, from the tiniest parakeet, to horses, and even a monkey amidst the dogs and cats. The tender epitaphs are much more personal than one will find in most human cemeteries.

Somehow, the loss of one's pet opens areas of the heart shielded by other moments in life. Some graves are adorned with pictures, some with toys, some with beautiful flowers.

Some are newly visited. Some are long left idle by owners who have since joined their beloved pets.

Few visitors were there on this cold, rainy day. My husband and I had only encountered one couple as we walked along the grounds.

Hartsdale covers quite a large space. One side of the cemetery faces a back road, and the main gates open out onto a busy avenue. From our vantage point, we could see a bus pull up and an old man get off and walk slowly into the cemetery. He carried a small, brown bag in his arms, no umbrella, and stopped to say "hello" as he walked by.

He told us the story of his little girl, a little white dog, and how he always came to visit her. You could feel the love shining in his eyes on this cold and grey day.

My husband and I did not interrupt his visit. She was buried near the gates. We watched him kneel beside her, leaving whatever was in his bag, and then we watched him walk out upon the avenue again.

After some time had gone by, my husband and I were concerned for this elderly man who still remained standing in the rain by the cemetery gates. My husband walked out through the gates and asked if he was okay and if he had a way to get home.

The man said that his son always picked him up but that maybe he had forgotten this day. My husband took out his cell phone, asked for the son's number, and called him.

Yes, he had forgotten; he would be right over.

In that cold and drizzly rain, I remember the beautiful graves, the beautiful epitaphs, and the beautiful peacefulness of Hartsdale. But I most remember that grey-haired, old man, walking through the rain to visit his dog. A dog he could never forget.

And the loyalty that a cold and drizzly rain could not wash away—loyalty, it seemed, even stronger than a busy son's memory.

Years have passed. I wonder if that grey-haired man and a little dog now roam Hartsdale's grounds together.

- Forty -
The Paths of Assisi

Some years ago, I had the good fortune to walk the peaceful paths of Assisi.

How could a place ravaged by earthquakes and persistent, blustery winds be so peaceful? Amidst the bustling winds and rubble of buildings damaged by quakes is a presence of peace palpable in the air.

It pervades the rubble, pervades the small passageways and mountain paths, and invades the spirit and heart. Walking Assisi forever changes each tourist.

The usual "touristy" shops lined the passageways and hillside of Assisi. St. Francis mugs and St. Francis postcards stare up at you as you walk by. But buying them did not feel right to me.

Mounted on walls of all the passageways were little boxes, donation boxes for the animals. And there were rescue dogs roaming the fields of Assisi.

I chose to bypass the St. Francis mugs and drop a donation in the box along the way.

Upon leaving Assisi, I was saddened that I did not purchase a "touristy" memento to take home.

Our next stop was the catacombs. As I walked into the gift shop, a beautiful little statue of St. Francis with the wolf looked up at me. I smiled and knew they would be coming home. And they have found a home on my bedroom bureau ever since, a reminder of the peace and sacredness of this mountainous place.

Part Four

Final Thoughts

- Forty-One -
Bringing Reiki Home

I thought I had made the worst mistake of my life. Reiki turned my world upside down.

As I said before, I had never been *normal*; I was always the one venturing out on the fringe. I was no stranger to energy. At the age of twenty, I almost died from electrocution. I feel that, due to this experience, my cells were forever modified to react and detect energy differently from that moment on.

I can feel auras. I have worked as an energy Intuitive, giving people guidance on which chakras of their bodies are out of balance. It enables me to detect supernatural energy, as well. My stories of paranormal encounters hold enough space for another book.

But, Reiki raised the ante to a much higher degree. My dogs sensed it immediately as I walked into my home. My sensitive sheltie, Apache Tears, so fearful of any change brought into her home environment, was beside herself with anxiety. She bit my husband that night. In my head, I kept chanting, "What have I done?"

I reached out to touch my husband's hand and felt Reiki. I was so distraught; I worried, "How do I turn this off? Is there no going back?"

No, there is no going back once you accept the Universe's energy into your life. But the physical body adjusts to it. Mine did. It was there, but it wasn't always starring center stage, unless I asked it to be. It was there, waiting in the wings, ready to provide endless energy to those who asked. I could hold my husband's hand as before. My dogs all accepted this energy as something natural and good. In the next few days, all was well.

So mesmerizing was this energy revelation that I progressed into higher levels and eventually became a Reiki Master. There are accelerated workshops that combine all teachings, but I don't recommend this. This would not have been a good way for me to experience and accept Reiki; the energy would have been too overwhelming. I am pleased that I took a slower approach with a wonderful teacher.

The night I came home from my second level of Reiki, I was, of course, apprehensive. But all was copasetic; the animals were at peace, and so was I.

That evening, at around two in the morning, I lay in bed awake in the dark. I held up my hands and saw my aura for the first time. Not a blazing glow, but a subtle, shimmering sparkle of light. I wanted to run out of bed and call my friend who had introduced me to Reiki and scream, "I see my aura." But I didn't.

I couldn't share all with my husband yet. He knew enough about my strange gifts, but as of yet, he did not fully comprehend them. As time progressed, he would watch as lines of people gathered to have me *read their auras* and walk away in amazement. He listened as I told them of medical issues which they were indeed struggling with in their lives. He still doesn't completely comprehend, but he believes there is validity to things we cannot "see."

My teacher sensed that I was hooked; she could tell the ones Reiki found. She told me that most people start and finish with the beginner's level of Reiki. Only a small portion continues on to become Reiki Masters, only the ones truly destined to channel Reiki to others during life.

Yes, Reiki found me; I only accepted the invitation. Thank you, Janie, for delivering that invitation to me.

- Forty-Two -
The Value of Reiki

It took me a couple of years to come to terms with a struggle which faces most Reiki Practitioners. It is a struggle over self-worth and monetary compensation. Reiki energy is free; it is an endless source of light. How can a price be placed upon it? Is placing a fee for Reiki right?

I had trouble accepting monetary compensation for Reiki. I volunteered and did many charitable functions. I met amazing people and animals along the way. Many people would repeatedly come to each charitable event and rave about my Reiki session but never schedule an office visit.

Maintaining an office is very pricey. This was a struggle I learned most Reiki practitioners deal with in their own lives. How do we charge money for something that is free, that is so benevolent and charitable? But how, then, do we maintain our livelihood as Reiki Practitioners?

I volunteered with an online organization of Distant Healers which sends Distant Reiki to animals and people, free of charge. I belonged to the animal network and met dozens and dozens of beautiful beings. We worked anonymously, never using the network as means of gaining financial profit for our own businesses.

I am so proud to have been a part of that organization; I met some of the most wonderful and caring people I have ever known. After I opened my own practice, it became harder to devote all the necessary time this organization required, but I shall never forget all the wonderful experiences and animals I met through my association.

A man heard about my Reiki practice and sent me an email about his aging horse. She had been fading. Her arthritic condition was escalating, seeming to sap her strength for life. I did a Distant Reiki and Animal Communication session with her and wrote to her owner what I sensed was contributing to her downfall. I told him she needed some sense of value in her life, that she wanted to continue working. I sensed she would be wonderful as a therapy horse, gentle with children. On the same day that I emailed the reading to him, two therapy organizations contacted him about utilizing his horse in their programs. She had been initially turned down by two other organizations, but her owner took a chance on these other options, and they reached out to him.

Coincidence? There are no coincidences in life, only doorways that open slightly. We may either turn the knob and open, or grasp the knob and shut.

I often gave my first session free of charge, as I did in this case. Helping this poor girl find purpose in life was my source of compensation.

Months later, this man reached out again on behalf of another sick animal. He told me he really didn't believe yet, but my "voodoo magic" worked once, so perhaps it could work again. Veterinary medicine didn't seem to be working.

I was truly torn here. I clearly sensed this man did not value my work or my time. I wrote back that, as usual, my first session was always complementary, but thereafter, I would be happy to arrange a schedule through my office for him. He never answered. I was right. To him, my "voodoo magic" and me were good enough for free but not worthy enough for compensation.

That incident shifted my consciousness. I realized that for people to truly value my work and worth, I had to first value them myself. The compensation I asked for was very reasonable. I still offer many free sessions and free readings when I feel the need to extend my help. My compensation is the appreciation and gratitude from those I have helped.

Getting people to appreciate the worth of Reiki is a challenge unto itself. Getting people to appreciate the worth of Distant Reiki is even harder.

Reiki and Distant Reiki hold the same intensity. Distance does not diminish the intent or strength of this energy. Many stories and testimonials from Distant Reiki sessions may be found on my website; they are truly heart-warming.

I have had pet owners tell me of such wonderful reactions to Distant Reiki. I always provide a specific time for my session to the owner so that they may have his or her pet in a relaxed, comfortable state. I don't want a pet outside playing ball when I send the energy. I wish him or her to be quiet and able to receive as much benefit as possible. However, even outside playing fetch, the Reiki would still be channeled.

Owners have said that pets receiving Distant Reiki would react as if the mailman had just come to the door—barking and jumping, then settling down as if to say, "All is okay. The energy is good." One pet owner said her little dog started jumping at her legs, in a state of agitation, before settling them. She said he seemed to be saying, "Hey, Mom, don't you feel this?" Sometimes, owners just say their pets are sleeping peacefully. It is so wonderful to sense the happiness in an owner's email, saying his or her pet ate better or seemed more interested in life the next day.

Reiki is not a miracle. When one's pet is meant to cross, Reiki will not interfere with the Universe's intention. But Reiki will help comfort and soothe and provide peace before the journey.

The most heart-felt letters of gratitude, written by owners after their pets have transitioned to the Bridge, will always be treasured by me. The most poignant ones are not posted on my testimonial page, as I value the privacy and heartache of these owners and wish not to publicize these words. But these words are valued more than any monetary compensation could ever be.

- Forty-Three -
Gratitude

I hope the pages of my book open the doorway of enlightenment a tiny bit wider for many of you reading of my experiences. Don't grasp the knob to shut; rather, turn the knob to open. There is such wonder waiting across the threshold.

The Universe is a wondrous place. Have the courage to step through and explore.

Explore within your own homes, using Reiki on your own pets, or continue the journey among others, as I have sought to do. I hope this book serves as a messenger to enlighten many others.

Reiki is meant to be shared; it is an endless source that strengthens with intention and does not diminish with use. The more steps you travel, the more you realize just how endless the journey of knowledge really is. There is always more to learn and share.

Thank you to all of the wonderful beings who have graced my path along the journey. You have all been wonderful teachers. I look forward to continued steps along the path and continued teachers waiting to share the wonder. Most of all, thanks to Reiki for *finding me* and carrying me across that threshold.

Namaste,

Shirl

Epilogue

I mentioned in the beginning of my book how childhood hurts can mold a person's life. My childhood was filled with hurt.

I was teased on a daily basis by cruel classmates because of my looks. I was very smart; others only sought me out for answers, and I wouldn't oblige, their use for me was done. I went home from school crying every day, not playing with friends, but rather quietly reading or painting in my room.

The worst day of my childhood came in sixth grade. A bully made a joke about me in class, causing a loud chorus of laughter to erupt. Among them was my teacher, laughing along. This was a teacher I idolized as a kid. We all wanted to be like our teachers back then. Seeing her laugh created a crack in my spirit that still has not been sealed.

But, hurt brings blessings. My closeness and gift with animals' spirits and souls has blossomed into Briar Rose, my Reiki practice.

Physical affection and praise were sparse in my home. Praise was handed out by an open wallet, not open arms. Good report cards were rewarded by a dress in every color hanging on the rack. I realize I was a lucky kid to have everything my parents could afford, but a spirit longs for things that cannot be bought.

That's a longing not easily outgrown. Today, I still buy *all the colors on the rack.*

This book is my clothes rack.

All the colors of the rainbow dwell in these chapters, encasing all the praise and worth I have sought in life, both as a child and as an adult.

Search whatever aisle or path in life that has all those colors for you. Sometimes, it takes decades to find it, to have the courage to paint a colorful picture or write a heart-felt story with all the hues.

Thanks for reading my story. Blessings in finding each of yours.

* * *

www.ingramcontent.com/pod-product-compliance
Lightning Source LLC
Chambersburg PA
CBHW022304060426
42446CB00007BA/451